LAURA

Laura

A True Story

Anonymous

CHRISTIAN PUBLICATIONS, INC.
CAMP HILL, PENNSYLVANIA

CHRISTIAN PUBLICATIONS, INC.
3825 Hartzdale Drive, Camp Hill, PA 17011
www.christianpublications.com

Faithful, biblical publishing since 1883

Laura
ISBN: 0-88965-207-4

02   03   04   05   06   5   4   3   2

You may be disturbed by my story.
It is not a casual read.
Although it deals with the unseen world,
I believe it provides answers to real needs.
My prayer is that you will be moved,
that you will begin to understand,
that you will praise a God who is able
to hold onto a life, a God who is able
to triumph through a life.

"You know how you play games at home?" my teacher asks, her eyebrows raised. Mrs. Brewster is very nice. She has short sandy-colored hair and her hands are soft.

"How many of you play games at home?"

Tommy sits next to me, and he raises his hand. Kim sits next to me, and she raises her hand. I don't raise my hand.

"You can play checkers or Parcheesi."

The teacher wants us to think about the last time we played a game together with our family. I'm thinking of one of the games we play in our house. My older brother and his friends play a game with me and his gun. They are very tall as they circle around me. Most of them are laughing. They come up close. Very close. I can smell them. I can smell the gun as someone puts it up to the side of my head. It smells oily. It smells smoky the way a gun smells after it shoots.

I think I can hear the sound of the trigger being squeezed. I can hear my heart jumping. I blink when the click comes and look quickly to see if I can still see. If you are dead, you only see black. This time I'm not dead. Each boy takes a turn. If the gun doesn't go off, he gets to take me as his wife. Then it's the next boy's turn.

"Aren't games fun?" the teacher smiles and asks. She has very straight white teeth lined up in her smile.

Tommy tells how he likes to play capture the flag outside at home with his dad and two older brothers. They run and try to tag each other. I don't like it when I'm being chased. I can never run fast enough. Maybe someday I will be able to get away.

Kim plays old maid around the table with her mom and dad. They have fun, she says.

I'm thinking of another game my father and Rudy play with me. Usually they drink a lot of beer first. Then they make a game of trying to smother me. They put the square pillow from the couch over my face and hold it there. I smell the dust that has collected in the crocheted cover on the pillow. I smell a musty smell. I smell beer. I hear giggling. One time; two times; three times. Then they leave me alone. The game is over for now.

"What other games do you play at home?"

Everyone in my class is eager to tell. Tommy and Kim and the others raise their hands and tell the whole class about their games. I just watch them talk. I don't raise my hand. They smile and tell Mrs. Brewster how much fun it is.

I just watch.

I am wondering.

Why are their games so different?

Why are their lives so strange?

Why aren't they like me?

Maybe it's because they are Americans.

Maybe they don't speak two languages at home—one to the old people and English to everybody else.

They are strange.

They cry when they take a tumble off the monkey bars on the playground. Sometimes they even scream if they see blood on their scraped knees or elbows. They cry and cry even after the teacher comes and hugs them. They don't stop until a long time later. I stand a little ways away and watch them.

Why do they cry so much?

I don't cry anymore.

When I am hurt or see blood, I just make myself a stone inside and stare with my eyes. It's better that way. It keeps the hurting things from hurting more.

Last summer when we were at the stock car races, someone accidentally spilled scalding coffee on my bare feet. I didn't cry then either. I just watched as the bright red part turned into a big, fat water blister. It hurt, but I was already a stone.

The other kids in my class aren't stones inside like me. They are different. They're afraid a lot too, but not the same way as I am. Some of the girls are afraid to walk across the metal bridge over the stream on the way to the other school building. The water below scares them. They cry, and sometimes Mr. Renner, the gym teacher, carries them across the bridge.

I'm not afraid of that.

I'm afraid I might die soon.

Kim is very much afraid of the dark. I'm not afraid of the dark. I'm afraid of who is in the dark. They tell everyone about being afraid. I tell no one. I just listen. They're afraid that something is going to happen to them. I'm afraid that what has already happened to me will happen again.

All those kids out there in my class have such strange ways. They pout to get their way. They get mad and sad and glad all in a row. They cry wet tears and laugh and are wild. I'm happy sometimes, too, on the outside part of me. But something is different.

Their lives are not like my life. They don't have hidden things. I'm always afraid that I am going to accidentally tell somebody at school or give them a clue. I'm afraid they're going to see the marks and know. I'm afraid that when I'm telling my lies about what happened, I will get mixed up and I won't remember how I told the story the first time. Then I might make a mistake and tell it differently the second time.

I mustn't tell. Never. Ever. Or I will get my "reward" from my father, the payment for telling. If I ever tell anyone about the hidden things, the games we play at home, my father makes it very, very clear what he will do to me.

"Don't tell, or I'll peel your skin off with a knife," he hisses through his clenched teeth.

He holds each of my small arms tightly in his big hands and lifts me up off the ground as he speaks. As I look up into his fiery, squinting eyes, I know that he will do as he promises. I have a clear picture in my mind's eye. My brother sometimes skins the squirrels and rabbits he brings back after hunting. So I know what I will look like if I ever tell.

If you stare at something long enough with your eyes, you can still see its outline even after you've looked away. My mind is so imprinted with the horror and terror of what awaits me if I dare tell that my stomach makes itself into a hard knot. My mouth itself becomes my enemy. I'm afraid that it won't stay quiet. Maybe sometime it will rush out past my pretend face and give away my secrets, my hidden things. Once before my mouth escaped.

"I was sick last night," I hear it telling Mrs. Brewster. I know what my mouth is going to say next. The thoughts are lined up in a neat row on the runway inside my mind. It's planning to say, "My stomach got squished when he jumped on top of me, and I got sick." But my mouth doesn't get a chance to betray me.

Mrs. Brewster's voice begins, "Oh, really? Well, we're going to have a lot of special things to do today. We're going to have art class, and then we'll have a special surprise this afternoon. I'm glad you came to school even though you felt a little sick. I'm sure you'll feel better today."

Why won't she listen to me? Can't she hear the screaming in my head? Doesn't she know? Doesn't she want to know? Part of me is mad at her. Why can't she see that I'm crazy? I went crazy when I was three. She must know that. Why won't she listen to me? She only tries to make me happy. She tries to make all the kids happy.

Tommy came to school mad yesterday because he had to eat oatmeal for breakfast instead of his favorite cereal. She tries to cheer him up just like she tries to cheer me up. But I'm not thinking about cereal. I'm trying to keep the volcano inside of me from erupting. I don't want them to do what they do to me anymore. I don't want to pretend to be happy. I want to scream. I want to tell her. I want her to listen.

Someday I'm going to find where my brother keeps his gun, and I'm going to take it to school. I'm going to go right into the classroom while the teacher is sitting at her desk. I can see the picture clearly in my head as I imagine what will happen. She has a pencil in her hand, and she is checking papers. We're all supposed to be working quietly. I'm going to go up to her and put the gun up to her head, right above her ear. Then she will listen to me. She will listen to me because she will have to listen to me.

Mrs. Brewster's hands are soft. She doesn't make quick moves. She only moves slowly when she comes by me. She never jerks me, and she never pinches me behind the neck with her thumb and finger. She never pulls my head back by my hair. She is never crazy. Her eyes never change. Her perfume smells very pretty, like bright spring flowers. She puts hand cream on sometimes in the morning at her desk. She lathers her hands together and brushes her cheek with the leftover cream.

She has fingernails that aren't farmer-lady nails. They are very long and curved, and they have shiny, clear nail polish on them. She doesn't look like she works in the barn or the garden because her nails aren't dirty. They're just round and pink and shiny. Someday I might wear nail polish. Someday my nails won't have farm dirt under them.

Maybe my teacher will want to take me home to live with her.

Maybe she has a cat.

I could play with it while she works on school papers.

I bet she has lots of food at her house.

Maybe she would be nice to me.

Maybe she would like me.

I like Mrs. Brewster. I like school. I like the second grade. But I'm afraid I won't be able to keep up at school. I have bleeps. A bleep is when you have a missing space in your head. It's like blinking, only you keep your eyes closed an extra-long time. While they are closed, people around you move. They even change seats. Sometimes they even change days. One minute you're looking out the window while Mr. Rogers is leading singing class. When you look back into the room, Mr. Rogers is gone. No one is singing. Everyone has his math workbook open to page six.

Where am I?

Who am I?

I look down at my desk and see that even I have page six open. The name penciled across the top of my paper in leaning letters is "Laura." I must be Laura. Now I remember. I'm Laura. Where do I go while my mind is asleep?

One

Who keeps being me while I am away?

What happens during the bleeps?

I don't know.

"How about number three, Laura?" The teacher and the class turn their heads and look at me.

Not yet. Just let me remember who I am for a little while longer. Am I supposed to know the answer?

Help.

Think.

Think.

Make your mind quiet.

Concentrate.

What is the teacher asking me?

Please. . . . Please. . . . Shh. . . .

My eyes dart back and forth as I try to be me again.

Laura.

Laura.

My name is Laura. I am in school.

That's Tommy over there.

I know who Tommy is.

It's like getting distracted and forgetting what you were saying in the middle of your sentence. You try hard to remember. You search your mind to make sense of what time it is now and what you were saying, what you were thinking, what the teacher is asking.

Bleeps make me tired. I have to do lots of thinking to remember who I am when I come back from my silent place inside my head. I never know when a bleep will come. I only know when one has already started. The volcano inside starts to erupt right before I leave, and my mind takes over. I can feel the pressure getting bigger and bigger, but I can't stop it.

Please help me, God.

Je-sus loves me! this I know,
  For the Bible tells me so.
Lit-tle ones to Him be-long;
  they are weak but He is strong.

Please God, help me glue my mind together again. Please.

Things are missing in my head. Everyone else in class seems to know things that I have never learned. I don't know how to add numbers. At least not all of them. I only know up to sixes and a little bit of sevens. Somehow I missed the rest. Probably a bleep came. I try to catch up, but it's so confusing. It's like my mind can't learn the things I'm trying to teach it. Parts are missing somewhere, and it refuses to keep learning until those parts are filled in again. But I have a good brain. Eventually it will let me learn again. When the volcano inside goes back down and things are quieter, then I can think better.

But for now we are drawing pictures.

Mrs. Brewster wants to see only happy pictures. Everything in school is too happy. Tommy and Kim draw yellow-crayoned pictures of their dogs and their families and their vacation and their nice houses. In my head I draw a different picture. On the left side of the page is a picture of me. My hand has been cut off. It's high up in the air, and blood is dripping down from it.

I make a black line in the middle of the paper going from the top to the bottom. On the other side, opposite me, is a picture of my father. His head has been cut off. His mouth is open big and wide the way it always is. And his head is rolling right off his body. I'm standing there with a knife in my right hand. I'm smiling. That's the kind of picture I want to draw. I don't want to draw stupid pictures of flowers and stupid pictures about going to the beach and stupid pictures about getting on a bus and going somewhere happy.

My eyes watch. They watch the teacher. They watch the other kids. They look to see how to be. I'm a very nervous person inside, but outside I pretend to be very quiet. I have an outside person and an inside person. The outside one is calm and quiet and laughs with the other kids and has fun.

"A joy to have in class—very helpful," the teacher wrote this time on my report card.

Inside is the screaming person, the nightmares, the daymares, the blackness. Inside is black and red. Outside there is a pretend white color. Inside is wanting to tear my hair out and beat my head with my fists. Everything is all right on the outside, and everything is all wrong on the inside.

I wonder if they can tell that I'm crazy?

* * * * *

We're having history now. Mrs. Brewster is standing by her charts and maps. They all roll up neatly at the top, and she can choose which one she wants to bring down for us to see. They are pretty maps, with each state a different color. The water parts are deep blue. But my mind can't see the maps. My ears can't hear the teacher talking. Only my eyes are busy. They are staring at the wooden rod the teacher is holding. She is using it as a pointer.

"Can anyone tell me the name of this state?"

She taps the map with the tip of the pointer, and the sound echoes in my head. Only it's louder. Much louder. And it comes again and again.

Stop. Stop.

I want to cover my ears.

I want to hide.

I want to run.

Something about her wooden stick terrifies me.

I try to keep my eyes busy. Maybe that will help. I study the desk I am sitting at. I make my finger follow the letters and shapes carved a long time ago into the wooden desktop. "J.T. + S.C." I trace the two long lines that circle around the hole where the inkwell used to be. We don't use the inkwells now, but the hole is still there.

My eyes move to the bulletin board at the right of the blackboard. It has a cheery, bright-yellow, accordion-like edge all along the sides. The yellow smiling bees in each of the corners look up and smile at me. Their smiles seem out of place. This is a sad place. A scary place. Why are they smiling?

My eyes find the green cards stretching out above the blackboard. They have two white lines going across them like railroad tracks. They have A B C D on them in cursive. There is a big A and a little a, a big B and a little b. . . . Up, down, up, down, up, down, up, down; one, two, three, four; one, two, three, four. Up, down, up, down, up, down, up, down.

Keep your mind going. Maybe it will help.

Shh. . . . You can be quiet now.

Don't be afraid. It will be all right.

I can see the house from my tree. "My artist tree," I call it. It's a perfect oval shape, like an artist would paint. It surprises your eyes as you scan the flat field it lives in. There are no other trees there. Only my tree. In fall its leaves turn orange, yellow, red. In the spring heavy seed-helicopters corkscrew to the ground when the wind catches them. It has been here keeping an eye on things here at the farm for a long time. My arms can barely reach halfway around the rough bark of its trunk. It stands on a little raised clump of ground high enough to watch everything.

I can see the house from my tree. If you're a good climber (and I am), it doesn't take much to climb up by grabbing onto the lowest branch and walking your feet up the trunk. There's a perfect sitting place up under the umbrella of green leaves. No one can see me here—unless I dangle my legs down. I can see everything that happens at my house.

It is my waiting place. I can see Rudy's big green car leave the driveway in a cloud of blue smoke. I can see my father walk out to the barn. I can hear him calling the cows in for milking. Sometimes the cows are bunched together under my tree, hiding—like me. But they're only hiding from the hot sun or trying to escape all the flies that pester them. Some stand, some lie with their front legs tucked up under them, catlike. I can hear their teeth crunch together as they chew their cud and rest in the cool shade of my tree.

I'm up here in my hiding place waiting. Waiting for Part A to return. Sometimes after I've been hurt by Rudy or someone else, I can barely swing myself up into my tree. My stomach hurts, or my legs are shaking. But the tree is a good distance from the house, and the walk across the field helps me begin to be alive again. I'm like a yo-yo going down, then up. I'm dead inside, then alive. Terrified, then all right. Part B comes with all its bizarreness. Then Part A, the sane part, returns. I'm waiting for Part A to return now.

My mind helps me change gears. The memory of the brutality that has just happened is already beginning to fade. If I try to keep Part A and Part B in my head at the same time, there isn't room. It makes me too confused. So I let my mind fill itself with happy things, small things: the soft wind moving the leaves; the cotton-ball clouds sailing happily from right to left in the bright sky; the lime-green inchworm hunching himself up the underside of the branch near me. Little things, nice things—things that seem to fill my mind so much that there is no room for reminders of Part B.

I don't want to remember.

My mind is doing the best it can.

It has to keep changing speeds.

Sometimes when the horrible nightmares of the day are happening, my mind goes extra slow, as though things are suddenly too much to take in all at once. Later, like now, as I watch from my tree, my mind goes its regular speed again. It's hard to keep changing speed, but it seems the only way to keep from going crazy.

As I sit here high up, I'm not trying to make sense of things. I'm only waiting—waiting for clues that I can go back to the house. I am waiting for the cloud of wickedness—the cloud that Rudy or any of my father's other friends bring with them—to leave. They come with a filth that seems to stay behind in the house long after they're gone. Lust is a dirty thing. It always seems to leave some of its stain on me when the men are through.

I don't ask why I sit up here in my tree. I can only remember asking it once when I was very small. My mind goes back to that time.

I'm only three years old. It's the first time my father takes me as his wife. I remember the hateful eyes, the strange look that comes over his face. In terror, I run to bury my face in my mother's skirt. I remember the feeling as she tries to pry my short fingers open one at a time so I will let go of her dress. I remember her pushing me away from her toward him. I remember the look of deadness in her face. I remember the stiffness in my body as I fight to get free. I remember the confusion. I remember asking "why" with my eyes.

When it is the first time for terror, you're surprised. It has never been like this before. You're not expecting it. You have no way of knowing what is about to happen. You wonder why. Why is he hurting me? Why this? But now I'm no longer surprised. I know now. I know that no one will help me. I know that there is nothing I can do to stop it from happening. I know that it is the darkness inside of them that rules them now. I know that somehow I must survive. I must never let them win. I know that each time it happens, it will end soon. I know that it will also happen again. Probably soon.

Sometimes I try, as I sit up here in my tree, to imagine how it would be to have a candy-coated life—a life without the awfulness; a life without physical pain; a life without the terror that the darkness brings; a life without the inner deadness I feel even now as Part A begins to come back into focus. I don't long for that kind of a life—I only wonder what it would be like.

Longing means you have hope left that maybe it will change. But I know that it won't change. The awfulness of Part B will always be in the shadows, waiting to rush forward to take me. It will always be there ruining the good parts of Part A; always reminding me that it's only behind the curtain, waiting for the right moment to once again reach out and grab me.

It's safe now. I can come down from my tree. The sensing inside me knows, as I watch my father begin the chores, that Part A has returned. He is in his right mind again. When I join him in the barn we will not speak of the atrocities of the afternoon. He won't even have to pretend he knows nothing about them. Somehow he will have completely forgotten them. His mind, like mine, has no room for such memories. He buries them somewhere deep inside and refuses to think about them.

As we work together, my father is himself again. His eyes are his own. Part A is here now. That's how he always is in his normal part. But he has a bomb inside, ready to go off at any moment. It doesn't take much to make the bomb explode—my being too slow, my not being strong enough to do something, my being dumb. The bomb goes off, and his rage erupts with a loud blast.

He slashes at me with his words.

"Can't you do anything right?"

"Don't be such a fool!"

Or, "I didn't ask for this tool, stupid!"

He punctuates his disgust by flinging the tool I have just handed to him across the barn. I'm not frightened by these outbursts of rage. In Part A, even in his anger, he never touches me. "That's just how he is," my mother explains to me.

On his especially bad days, she warns me to stay out of his way so I won't do something stupid and make him yell. I don't hate him because he yells a lot; that's just how he is. Mostly it's my fault that he is that way anyway. I do a lot of stupid things to aggravate him.

Sometimes he starts one of his harangues, as I call them. Something my mother does or I do enrages him. He explodes in a rage of words that keeps going on and on. Sometimes he rages for a half hour, sometimes an hour, pacing back and forth and gesturing in quick movements with his hands. Sometimes I return to the book I'm reading as he paces in front of my chair. He doesn't seem to notice that I'm not listening. Once I even walked back into my bedroom as he raved. He followed behind me and kept his anger alive, while I worked away cleaning my room.

When his rage tires, he leaves the house, slamming the back door as he stalks out to the barn or the fields. I have never heard him apologize. When he returns, he seems to have forgotten how we have aggravated him so.

In Part A, I would describe him this way: my father is a hard worker who has a bad temper. The people at church never see his temper. The people at the factory never see his temper. But I see his temper very, very often. His temper is safe unless his eyes change. Then the darkness comes. Then I die a little more inside as the horrible part returns.

Don't be afraid.

It'll be all right.

* * * * *

Tonight my mind has its movie going again. I don't want to watch, but I can't turn the images off. My mind machine insists on clicking past the scenes of the day over and over and over. My nose takes part in the movie too, just like my eyes do. It smells and remembers. Even my ears do their part to fill in the sounds that fit with each picture frame. My eyes try to look away, but these pictures are embedded in my mind. Once they are there, you can never be sure they will stay quiet, hidden away where they belong.

At night the pictures tumble down as though someone had thrown a pile of memories high up in the air. They flutter down into a scattered mess on the floor, one on top of the other. Not whole pictures. Not long scenes. Only a snapshot here, a frozen frame there. Not in proper order, but a disorganized slide show of scraps of the day or of the week—a closeup of a silent screamer, eyes closed, mouth open wide; hands tied behind a back; red water; the woody smell of beer; the rough sandpaper stubble on a bony face; the sound of a fist meeting a face, a mouth, an eye; heavy breathing; a frightening glimpse of a wicked, leering face; hot things coming closer to an arm; dirt under long uneven fingernails of a calloused hand.

Pictures.

Memories.

Reminders of the day from Part B.

I can't stop the movie in my mind as I lie here on my bed. It's reliving what I have already started working to forget. From deep inside the screaming grows louder and louder as my mind shows reruns. I can't stop the pictures, but I do know how to quiet the screaming. I know how to make myself forget. My bed is pushed up against the wall. I lay on my side with one hand tucked up between my pillow and my face. That hand hides there as my other one reaches out to touch my friend on the wallpaper.

Sometimes the ridges of old nail holes interrupt the smoothness of the wall as my fingers go around and around. Circles. Slow tracings around the quiet farmer lady etched on the wallpaper. She is my friend.

My fingers do their work for an hour or more. They are my eraser. They smooth over the terror that fills the inside. They trick my mind into forgetting. They distract the screamer by the patterned rhythm of their movement. Again and again. Around and around. They stop the pain inside, quiet the anguish. Help me forget.

Hold me, Jesus.

* * * * *

The picture I see every week on the Sunday school wall fills my mind just now. It's one of Jesus with a little lamb straddling His strong neck. Jesus' face is filled with softness, kindness, love. His eyes seem to look straight at me. His hands make sure the lamb doesn't slip backwards off His neck.

They are strong hands.

Hands that protect you.

Safe hands.

The lamb is snuggled up as close to Jesus as it can be. Its head rests down a little on His shoulder. Its body feels the warmth of the Savior.

It is safe.

It is quiet.

It is Jesus' little lamb.

Hold me, Jesus.

I don't see Him, but I can feel His arms around me. He draws me toward Himself as I lie there in the darkness on my bed. His strong arms make a circle around me. My face nestles down into the softness of His chest, and I am comforted. I don't have to tell Him what they have done to me. He seems to already know. The lady on the wall helps me forget. But Jesus helps me remember whose lamb I am.

I belong to Him now.

I decided when I was seven.

"Some of you boys and girls here don't know the Savior."

The words of the visiting pastor with the kind eyes reach me as I sit on the hard wooden pew. My legs dangle over the edge and pulse back and forth as I silently kick the air. I don't look up, but I'm listening.

"Just because your moms and dads are Christians and you come to church every Sunday, that doesn't mean you yourself are a Christian. You'd better be sure."

With the simplicity and honesty of a seven-year-old, I talk to God later in my room.

"I'm not sure, God, if I'm a Christian or not. But if I'm not, I want to be. I believe, like the pastor said, that You died for my sins. I want You to be my God."

Everything changed.

Everything.

In my black and white world, I have just agreed with the white side, the side of the Light. Up until now, I've known that I didn't want the dark side. I've seen that side often in my father's eyes. But as I write on the first page of my Bible in carefully printed letters: "I was saved on March 7, 1954," I know everything is different.

I belong to Him now.

"My G___, what happened to your face?"

My father cradles my bruised face in his big hands. I can taste the familiar taste of blood in my mouth. My tongue runs along my top row of teeth checking for any missing ones. No spaces. Good. This is one of the times when Part A and Part B of my life collide. My world crashes in a confused swirl.

I used to be more confused. Now I have learned that life doesn't have to make sense. My mind doesn't have to be able to figure out what is going on, what has just happened. Then and now rarely match. Don't try to explain how Part A and Part B fit together. You can't. They don't. Life is not on a continuing line. Yesterday has nothing to do with today. Don't try to make sense of your life. Just live it and try to figure out what you should do in the now part.

My father's shocked words and genuine concern are part of Part A, the sane part. What he himself has just finished doing to me is part of Part B, the crazy part. That's all the explanation I need.

Much of the anguish inside is there because there are two parts to my life. If it were only Part A, I could make sense of it. If there were only Part B, I could make sense of it. Together, it doesn't make sense at all. Many years ago I quit trying to make my life fit into what my mind said it should be. I was only four years old then. Life was too big to make sense of for such a little girl.

"Who did this to you?"

My swollen eyes only let me peek out through small slits. My father has crouched down next to me as he reaches forward with his hands. I must have fainted again. I only remember being pinned against the wall by the crazy, raging man who now touches me with such tenderness. I must have fallen here with my back against the dining room wall.

I watch in silence the face so close to mine. My memory is full of pictures; my body is full of pain. But my father has no memory of what has just happened. His confusion and horror want me to explain, to point the finger at the brutal one who has left me in this condition. But my mouth refuses to speak—not from fear or confusion, but because it has nothing to say. There is no way I can find words to tell my father something that his mind refuses to remember anyway.

I study his face. Hints of the red-flushed look he had just a few minutes ago are still seen on his face. I can still smell the beer on his breath. For a minute my throbbing face wants to feel the warm, tender touch of his two hands on my cheeks. But from somewhere inside a sense of terror forbids me to be comforted by those hands.

Don't trust him.

Don't accept his love.

Don't be fooled by his tenderness.

My father has a crack in his head.

That's how I always explain it to myself. I'm talking about what happens when the window of my father's mind changes and a curtain comes over his face. The curtain is the craziness. The curtain is the darkness. The curtain is the bizarre man my father becomes as Part B of my life rushes to the front.

Sometimes, as the change occurs, it seems as though there's a moment in time when his face reflects half and half—the half of the normal part when he is in his right mind and the half that has the wild, demonic look. It's as though a crack runs down the length of his face and he, for a split second, remains as two different men.

My father has a crack in his head.

I've seen it happen so many times that I don't even watch it with curiosity anymore. Always, after the momentary stillness while the change occurs, there is a new presence, a new sense of the darkness. It's as though a cold, chilling wind has swept through the room. There's the knowing that even though you see no one, there is someone, something, present with you now who was not there before.

Terror.

Wickedness.

Fear.

Violence.

Blasphemy.

Blackness.

Death.

Destruction.

The presence of all are felt as the darkness takes over in the body of the man I know as Father. He becomes another. The look he now has in his eyes gives away his choice. He has chosen the darkness. His eyes become piercing, hateful eyes, with the haunting look of death around the edges.

The rest of his face undergoes the same change. The mouth seems first to move down a little, and then an unearthly sneer

21

curls the lips back. It reminds you of the way a dog's lips pull back when he snarls. The entire face takes on the look of someone—something—else. The change has already begun now as I slump back against the wall. The tenderness and concern in my father's eyes are replaced by the steel glare. The questioning mouth is replaced by a mocking jeer.

"What happened to you, my dear? Did you take a fall and hurt yourself?"

The voice that speaks is no longer that of my father, at least not Part A of my father. It's deeper, more guttural, more not of this world. It's his other voice. I know it well. It has mocked me often before.

As I stare up at the eyes, I'm not afraid. There is a terror that grows so big that it turns back on itself and refuses to show any feeling of fear, any trembling. I am already a stone. I already don't care anymore. I already have died on the inside.

"Let's make your other eye look the same color."

The viciousness, the power of the new person in front of me does not come as a surprise. I know what happens to me after my father has a crack in his head. I know that the only way to survive now is to blank out all the physical pain and refuse to give in to the darkness. They know I am in the light now. The spiritual beings that seem to fill the air around me know that I am not one of them. They were listening in my room as I sat on my bed and chose which side I was on. The presence of a new Spirit within me is evidence of to Whom I now belong. That's why the darkness is trying so hard to destroy me.

As the blows come once more, this time with all the power of the darkness behind them, I feel nothing. At least for the moment I am far away somewhere up above myself. As I watch the beating going on, my mind quietly tells me that I cannot stand much more of this. Someday they will kill me. Someday should come today. Then I would be at the end of all of this awfulness.

Please God, let me die.

Don't be afraid. It'll be all right.

* * * * *

"The B-I-B-L-E, yes that's the book for me. . . ."

I like going to Sunday school. I like memorizing verses so I can save up my red tickets and pick from the treasure chest. There is a cardboard bee in there. It has a rubber band across the bottom. If you swing the bee by its string, it buzzes like a real bee. Next time, I'm going to choose the bee from the treasure box.

"I stand alone on the Word of God, the B-I-B-L-E."

I like learning about the God I have chosen. I carry my almost-white Bible to church every Sunday. I like learning about how strong God is and how much He smiles. I get very sad when I learn about the things that make Him sad. He gets sad when I disobey Him. He is sorry because sin is bad. He teaches me lots of things. He is my best friend.

I pray to Him a lot. I pray about the people we hear about in our missionary flannel graph stories in Sunday school. Some of them are hurt by evil people in faraway places because they love the Lord Jesus. I know what that is like. I know how it is to be hurt, to be mocked because you will not agree with the darkness. I understand. I pray for them to be able to be strong against the darkness. I know all about things like that.

I'm learning in Sunday school about how Christians are supposed to act. We learn something new each week. I want to learn to be good.

"Do any of you boys and girls ever fight with your brothers and sisters?" Mrs. Richards, our second-grade Sunday school teacher, has a serious look on her face. Our Sunday school room is small, even for only the six students seated around the low table. We're resting our elbows on the tabletop. Our chins are in our hands as we look up at the teacher.

"Some brothers and sisters even hit each other or scratch with their fingernails. Have any of you ever done that?"

Most of us have a quiet, guilty look, and then a few nod with serious conviction. I watch the others and then nod too. I am remembering how I scratched my older brother the last time he and his friends came to take me as their wife. It doesn't usually make any difference if I resist or not, but I always fight anyway. A desperateness floods over me as I realize it is beginning again, and I lash out. Yesterday, as they all came to take me, I scratched a big, thin line down my brother's cheek.

"Jesus hates it when we fight with our brothers or sisters. He calls it sin."

I like Mrs. Richards. She is a kind teacher who sometimes lets the boys get a little out of control during the class. She knows God really well. She tells all of us what Jesus says, what Jesus thinks, what makes Him happy, what makes Him sad.

"Boys and girls, let's tell Jesus right now that we are sorry for fighting with our brothers and sisters and promise that we will try not to do it again. Then today, when you go home, why don't you tell your brother or sister that you are sorry for fighting with him or her. That would make God very, very happy."

Mrs. Richards drags out the "verys" for emphasis. We all bow our heads as she leads us in a prayer of confession, a prayer of promise, a prayer of being sorry.

I don't pray. At first a hint of confusion passes through my mind. How could God be mad at me for scratching my brother when he was trying to do those awful things to me? It doesn't make sense. Why did the teacher say that? I don't understand. I guess it's one of those things I just can't figure out.

Many times before, there have been things in my life that I can't make sense of, things that don't fit together. At those times I always do the same thing. Somehow God has given me an ability just to leave unexplained those things that don't make sense. It's as though there is a special place in my thinking where confusing things can go without disrupting the rest of my thoughts. I don't try to make sense of them. I just put them in the special resting place for the unexplained.

Many things are there, in my resting place inside. One of them is something Mrs. Richards told us. She said that God answers prayer.

"He will always, always hear you, and He will always, always answer. When you have a problem or are afraid, pray to God. He will help you with your problem. He will help you not to be afraid."

That makes sense to me. I know Jesus is the Shepherd God, the God of the Bible, the God who has only recently become my God. I'm going to try to do as Mrs. Richards says. I'm going to pray, and God will answer me. He will help me.

* * * * *

Now I'm at home. It is night. As I lie here on my bed listening for the footsteps of the men, I do as the teacher said we should do. I come with my childlike faith. "God, don't let the men come for me tonight. Don't let them hurt me. Help me not to be so afraid." But it doesn't work.

The men come anyway.

They hurt me anyway.

I am afraid anyway.

I don't know it now, but it will be three decades before God will explain why He hasn't answered, why He is so silent. All I know now is that He hasn't answered my prayer. But, as the dark presence I feel around me and the mocking voices within scoff at my childish faith, God puts the same words into my heart that He has often placed there before. Somehow He plants a simple faith within me that speaks out against the darkness.

"I don't understand, but I still choose Him."

Maybe it is because there are only two colors in my world. There is the black, and there is the white. I've always known that there are really only two choices, only two gods—the God of the Bible (the Creator God) and the god in the sky (the black prince). If I stop loving the One, there would only be the other left to serve. And I know all too clearly what that service includes.

I've been learning about the God I've chosen. He is kind. He is strong. He wants to help me. He is sad when the men abuse me. He cries with me at night, when only my cat knows about my tears. He hates what I hate about the darkness. He is the only One I have. He talks to me sometimes when I'm alone in bed at night—not in a voice that my ears can hear, but in a voice that my heart can hear.

Once He spoke to me when I was on the roof. I climbed there to get away from the awfulness. I'm balancing carefully on the metal part at the very top of the roof where the points meet each other. I'm walking toward the edge. I've decided to fly off the being alive part and fly into the being dead part.

I can't stand it anymore. I want to come and be with You, Jesus, in heaven. It's quiet there where You are, our teacher says, and there are no tears. It must be that no one hurts you there.

"What are you doing, Laura?" As I'm walking step by step toward the end of being alive, I hear His voice. I hear it inside my heart. I don't want to be alive anymore. I can't stand it the way it is. They say the darkness owns me. They say I belong to them.

I'm almost at the edge of the roof now, almost at the end of being alive, when I hear Him again.

Laura, they lie to you.

They don't own you.

You belong to Me now.

You are Mine.

You belong to Me now.

You belong to Me now.

You belong to Me now.

The words echo in my mind like a faraway voice reaching me at the bottom of a deep, dark well.

You belong to Me now.

I'm not alone!

I have a friend called Jesus.

He talks to me.

He hangs on to me.

He says I belong to Him now.

I love Him the most of anybody.

I belong to Him now.

FOUR

I lift the heavy hay bales as best I can, tossing or rather swinging them up onto the wagon. Only 150 acres, but days and weeks and years of hard work. Bad soil. Too many rocks. Not enough time with his factory job for my father to get everything done on the farm. But I like working outside. I can never remember doing inside chores—chores for girls like ironing, washing dishes, sweeping. I'm needed outside.

But I don't mind. I like working in the fields. I like the feel of the wind toying with my long hair, brushing it softly across my cheeks. I like the feel of the sun shining down on my bare arms and warming me up. I like the sweet smell of the new-mown hay as I ride high up on the stacked hay wagon. I like the feel of the soft brown dirt between my toes as I walk barefoot across the furrowed fields.

Dirt smells.

I like that smell.

I'm helping with the second cutting of hay now. I wrestle the bales of hay off the ground. The cut ends poke through my thin slacks and leave little scratch marks in a rash above my knees. I toss them up over my head as best as I can, and

29

my brother snags them with the worn metal hay hook he holds in his right hand. The itchy hay dust showers down on me like a sudden mini snow squall.

Every half hour or so I need to turn aside and vomit as my stomach complains about such heavy lifting. My father's stomach insists in the same way that the work is too hard even for him. I come back to my lifting.

A storm is coming. From up here on the top of the hill I can see the veil of misty rain sliding like a shower curtain across the valley below. The sky in the distance is grayish-black. Lightning flashes like rough edges of broken glass crashing to the ground. We have to get all the hay in before the storm comes. Work faster. The wind that comes ahead to announce the rain makes it hard for me to see. It drapes my long hair over my face as I bend to struggle with the bales.

Hurry.

Work faster.

It is too fast.

It is too hard.

It is too much for my little muscles.

Now the wagon is full. The field is empty. I walk stiffly into the house and lay down on the dirty carpet in the living room. I don't mind the dusty smell or all the dog hairs. I only want to rest. My arms and legs are quivering, still somehow trying to be strong.

As I lie here, everything seems to stiffen up even more. Sometimes I stay stretched out on the floor until after bedtime. I ache. My father works himself and also works us with a fever and speed that says you can get your body to do anything if you really want to. Work is the important thing.

Part A.

Hard work.

Heavy work.
A swim in the creek.
Hay.
Wheat.
Pigs.
Cows.
Milking.
Busy.
Tired.
Not unlike my friends' lives. The normal part.

* * * * *

It's Thursday again.
Rudy's day.
After bowling.
$2.
Always the same.
$2.
Rudy puts it down on the table. Sometimes he pays in shiny half-dollars piled up in a neat stack. Sometimes he pays in crumpled, old-smelling green bills. I hate the smell of money. My father is in no hurry to pick it up tonight. He keeps drinking his half-warm cup of coffee.
$2.
It's time. Rudy is in kind of a hurry tonight. He skips the two or three beers he usually drinks beforehand with my father. My father looks at me and jerks his head to the side, toward Rudy. It's time.
The short hallway that ends in my room seems to be a long one tonight as I follow Rudy. My stomach is already remem-

bering, already hurting. I shouldn't have eaten so much spa-
ghetti. I'll probably get sick. Why was I so stupid?

Rudy lifts the old heavy drape that covers my doorway. He
bows courteously with his hand stretched out as his smile
mocks me. As soon as I go in past my drape, even before we
begin, I have trouble breathing. My mouth and lungs already
remember that it's usually hard to breathe. The rising sun
shapes at the head and foot of my metal bed frame are silently
waiting. Five pipes on each of the suns. I have counted them
often.

One . . . two . . . three . . . four . . . five.

One . . . two . . . three . . . four . . . five.

Most of my practice at being a stone inside happens when I
am with Rudy. Some of the men who pay the $2 are tall. Some
are fat. Rudy is short and thin. He has strong, bulging muscles.
He must have skipped bowling tonight. He doesn't have on his
bowling shirt. It has words on the back and his name on a
square in the front on his pocket. No, tonight he has on his work
clothes. They are the same dark gray ones my father and all the
other men at the factory wear to work each day. His black
slicked-back hair is dangling in a messy way over his forehead. I
don't like the way he smells—sweat, hair grease, beer, old aftershave.

Even before he ties my hands and feet to the rising suns, I
have already died inside. My arms are limp and quiet. They
don't belong to me anymore. Rudy has to tie me. He has to be
sure. More than once, if left untied, my arms are too frightened
to be still. My hands sometimes do bad things. My fingernails
leave uneven red lines down the side of Rudy's face as my lungs
fight to be able to breathe. When that happens, my father's eyes
fill with the wicked look that I know as the darkness. He will

teach me never to do that again. He rages at me each time Rudy is displeased.

Sometimes, so I will learn, my father shuts the closet door with only me on the inside. The lock scrapes as the key turns until the click comes. At first the darkness frightens me, and the screaming inside grows louder and louder. I sit quietly like an Indian with my legs crossed. My face brushes the clothes hanging silently in the closet as I rock forward and backward, forward and backward. The dresses hanging here are my friends.

I can smell the leather of high-heeled shoes lined up in a perfect row beside me. Soon the slit of yellow light drawn in a narrow pencil line under the door helps my eyes to see even in the blackness. I put my hand down in the pointed toe of the shoe closest to me. I pretend that it's walking. Tap, tap, tap. A pretty lady. A fancy dress. Sparkly jewelry. Tap, tap, tap. I am walking. I want to stay in here forever, in the dark. It is safe here. No one hurts me here. I have been put in the special closet many times.

But tonight, with Rudy, my hands will not do bad things. They can't. They are tightly tied to the rising sun, as are my feet. But perhaps my teeth will make trouble for me. Sometimes they leave little pictures of themselves in a neat circle on Rudy's arm. He likes to play his games. He likes to hear me scream. Screaming makes him laugh. He likes to see blood. Blood makes his eyes go even more wild. He begins to change. He welcomes the darkness. Rudy doesn't know it, but he's teaching me how to be a stone inside. I will not let him enjoy my screaming.

I will be silent.

He will not win.

He will never win.

As we start, I do what I always do. I float up silently in my mind to the ceiling. From my high-up place I can see Rudy abusing the blonde nine-year-old girl who is tied to the rising suns. I see her biting her lip to hold in the screams. Her face gets very red. I see her eyes staring up at me, wondering why I don't do anything to help her. She must not understand that there is nothing I can do to help her.

Some people have smiling, happy lives.

Some people have dirty, screaming ones.

She has the dirty kind of life.

He's asleep now next to me. His back is lying on the pile of drapes that I use as blankets. The top one is a worn green color with threads of white, then yellow, then red, then white again. I can hear Rudy breathing noisily, in and out. I can see his chest rise and fall. I can feel his arm touching my side as he sleeps beside me. I can smell the smell that is Rudy.

Please God, don't let him wake up. Then he will begin all over again. Lie still. Breathe quietly. Don't move. Maybe he will forget that he loves me. Maybe he will just get dressed and go away.

As Rudy sleeps, I come down from the ceiling, and my pretend friend on the wallpaper is waiting for me. The beautiful farmer lady busily feeds her chickens and waters her red flowers. Her long hair is tied back in a neat bun with a red ribbon to hold it in place. Her long flowing dress reaches to the ground, and the black tips of her pretty shoes peek out from under her skirt. She hums softly to herself, and her humming comforts me. She doesn't look up from her work as my hand reaches out to touch her.

My fingers make a soft, slow pattern around and around her. She is so kind. She is my friend. She is quietly happy as she works and lets me be close to her. She doesn't seem to have heard the muffled screams or to have seen the awful events, but she knows. She knows. She smiles and scatters grain for the yellow-beaked chicks gathered at her feet. She seems to say, "Don't think about that now. Look at my pretty flowers. Listen to my chicks peeping in their little scratchy voices."

Around and around.

The circles quiet the screaming inside.

She is my friend.

Don't be afraid.

It'll be all right.

y mother has done farm work all her life. Her father was a farmer. Her husband is a farmer. Her body tells you she has done heavy lifting, hard work, unfeminine jobs. She has that tired look that overworked people get. The sun has made the skin on her arms look like tough, tanned leather. The wrinkles are those of a much older woman.

Sometimes I study her hand as I sit next to her in church. I trace the faint blue lines of the veins that run like silent rivulets across the back of her hand. My mother looks down at me as I touch her hand. She smiles. I like my mother. She's nice to me. She's very gentle and kind. My mother loves God. She has a Bible in her own language and also one in English. She says that the words from her own Bible "ring in her heart."

She has never gotten used to going to the English-speaking church, to reading from the English Bible. It doesn't mean the same to her, she says. But she is a Christian. Her father and mother belonged to a church in the old country, but that church didn't teach the same things about Jesus as the English-speaking church does. The English church believes that you have to personally accept Jesus Christ as your Savior in order to get to heaven. My mother says she did that when she visited an English-speaking church one Christmas a few years ago. My father says he did the same thing too. But he still swears and yells a lot, even in the Part of his life before the darkness takes over.

My mother reads her Bible every day. If I get up really early, I see her kneeling in front of the sofa. She has her hands folded in prayer. I can't hear what she is saying, but I can see her lips moving. She's talking to the God of the Bible. She loves God, but she doesn't study the Scriptures the way our pastor says we should. She says that the Bible is too complicated to understand, so she reads only parts of it.

My mother has always been poor. Her parents were poor. Her husband is poor. When she can't afford to buy clothes for us, she bleaches the cream-colored cloth sacks we buy flour in and makes underwear for us. Sometimes the bleach only makes it part-way white, and I can still see the "Gold Medal" letters arching across the front.

My mother sews most of our clothes. She can make anything we need out of the drapes she buys at rummage sales. She doesn't even need a pattern. She just makes her own out of a brown grocery bag, drawing our outlines as we lie on the floor on top of the paper. She pins the pattern to the big stretch of drapery material and begins cutting. Sometimes she makes matching dresses for my baby doll too.

My mother is nice to me—most days. She is in her right mind—most days. But some days her "inside sister" comes forward. Mostly it's when my father comes home or after some of the men have been here in the evenings.

I hate her inside sister. She hurts me. Sometimes my mother is the person looking out at me from behind her eyes. Sometimes her sister is the one staring back at me. The eyes tell me who is there. They tell me if I should be afraid or not.

Five

My mother is nice to me, but her sister is mean to me.

My mother takes care of me as best as she can, but her sister gives me over to the scary men.

My mother loves the God of the Bible, but her sister hates Him.

My mother is gentle, but her sister is violent.

When my mother's sister comes, my mother gets very quiet. She hides away somewhere inside. She must be afraid of her sister. I am too. I can always tell when the change in my mother begins to happen. Her eyes are the first to give her away. At first I can still see a little corner of my mother left in her eyes. She's busy doing what she always does when her sister is near. She's making herself be like a stone.

A stone doesn't feel.

A stone can't hurt.

She has to be a stone when her sister comes.

Her sister takes over when things are too bad, too horrible for my mother to see. Her sister is more like a robot. She's a robot for my father. She does what he says. Her eyes match the darkness in my father's eyes. She serves the black prince just like he does. She sometimes curls my mother's lips back in a mocking sneer and says wicked things to me. When my mother's sister is nearby, she hates me.

"If you're not dead by the time you're twelve, I'll kill you myself!"

Maybe I should be sad when my mother says that, but I'm not. She doesn't say it; her sister does. I'm not sad, but I am afraid. What if my mother's sister is here when I'm twelve? What if my mother isn't the one looking back at me from behind her eyes? Who will help me? I'm afraid of my mother's sister. She lets the black prince take over in my mother's body.

Hold me, Jesus, hold me. I'm scared.

Sometimes when the bad things are happening, my mother comes by behind her eyes, then her sister comes, then my mother comes back again. They take turns being her. Usually, after everything is over, my mother comes to stay again until the next time. She never seems to remember. She never seems to have seen what my eyes have seen. She never asks questions. She never tries to piece things together. She just goes on with her life where it left off—before her sister took over.

Maybe she really knows what they have done to me, but she wants to pretend that she doesn't know. Maybe she feels very, very bad that those awful things are happening to me. Maybe she will protect me the next time.

Maybe.

Maybe not.

I only have one mother. The other one, her sister, is not really my mother. She must be a man, even though she is in my mother's body. Sometimes when my mother's sister is near, she acts like a man. Women are good, but they are for hurting. Men are strong. They do the hurting. Sometimes my mother acts like a woman; sometimes she acts like a man.

I wish I weren't a girl because girls are women when they grow up. I hate being a girl. Girls are like women. They are for hurting. If I were a man, I could be strong and stop bad things from happening to me and to my mother. Girls always get hurt. My brothers never get hurt. They only get yelled at a lot, but my father never touches them. But I'm a girl, so I get hurt. That's just the way it is.

God, why did You make me a girl instead of a boy? Didn't You remember what girls are used for? Maybe You forgot. Maybe You wanted me to be a girl, but You didn't want them to do those things to me. Maybe You are very mad at them for what they have done to me.

Maybe.

Hold me Jesus. I'm afraid.

* * * * *

I can see the dirt under his long, broken fingernails. His breath smells like my father's does when he visits me at night. He is my father's brother, Uncle Gus. I will not learn until many years later that men like Uncle Gus and my father are called "alcoholics."

Uncle Gus has sandy-colored strings of thin hair that try to cover a bald spot on the top of his head. His face is long and bony with sunken cheeks. His eyes have a bloodshot glazed look most of the time. Mostly I notice the prickly stubble of his beard. He's a good babysitter. My mother drives up his long muddy driveway and leaves me with him when she goes into town to shop each week. His wife is a maid in town, so she's not usually at home when Uncle Gus takes care of me.

He's a good babysitter.

My mother says so.

Maybe she doesn't know.

I sleep a lot when I visit Uncle Gus. He always gives me his special "pop," as he calls it, to drink as soon as my mother leaves the end of the driveway and heads out onto the paved road to town. His special pop has soap bubbles on the top. It smells like he does. It makes me spin inside my head, and Uncle Gus has to carry me to the bedroom or I will tip over when I try to walk.

Maybe she doesn't know.

My eyes study the blue and red lines in Uncle Gus' flannel shirt. The buttons are little pretend plastic logs that sometimes poke me as they push hard up against me. I stare hard at the cracks in the floor of Uncle Gus' bedroom. The wooden cracks go across the room, under the bed and up to the door. I study lots of things when I'm in bed with Uncle Gus. It helps me be somewhere else.

I have to keep secrets, or Uncle Gus will have to hurt his wife. He tells me many times how he will cut her arms and legs off with a butcher knife if I am bad and tell. Sometimes he calls me at my house. When my mother hears that Uncle Gus wants to talk to me, she hands the phone to me, and I listen. He reminds me about the arms and legs and the big knife he has. I don't say anything. I only listen. When he's done talking I hand the phone back to my mother, and she hangs it up.

Maybe she doesn't know.

The next time I watch her car drive away down Uncle Gus' lane, I wish very hard. I wish that my mother would not leave me with my good babysitter. I wish that she wouldn't have to go to town each week. I wish that I didn't have to study the lines in the floor, the lines on Uncle Gus' flannel shirt.

I wish she knew.

Maybe she does know.

Maybe she wants it this way.

* * * * *

"Our people are more spiritual than the Americans. We can see into the spirit world in ways they can't." My mother's statement is not one of empty pride. It's a fact.

This is another piece of Part A in my life. It's the invisible piece, the powerful piece, the piece I think everybody has. It's the psychic part, although I won't know to call it that until years later. It is the power within to go beyond the visible. It's a God-given power, or so we all believe. I use it every day. I see my mother use hers too.

Five

It is the ability to do everyday things; the ability to know who's calling on the phone even before I pick it up; the ability to look into my schoolteacher's mind and know a split-second before the rest of the class that she wants us to turn to page sixteen in our math books; the ability to know my mother is contacting me in my mind while I am at school, giving me reminder messages.

The power behind these abilities also helps me to predict the future. One time I announced that my aunt was going to arrive from faraway New Jersey in an hour. I wasn't surprised when she arrived exactly as predicted. I knew she was coming even though I'd never met her before.

I also have other abilities; the ability to make books or toys fly across the room when I get bored of staying in bed because I am sick again; the ability to know if a woman is going to have a girl baby or a boy baby. Like breathing or thinking or walking, everyone in our family has these abilities. All of my aunts have these abilities too. The people in our farming community know about them and often come to them if they need special help.

One of my aunts is a "finder." If you lose something, you pay her, and she dreams where you lost it. Another aunt is a "water witch." She has the ability to use a y-shaped branch from a tree to locate water under the ground. If you dig where she tells you, you always find water. My other aunt can talk to the dead. If you pay her, she will hold a seance and communicate with your dead husband or brother or mother.

The people who live near us know both of my grandmothers as "white witches." That means that they have abilities too, but they never use them to harm people. You can never pay them to cast a spell to hurt another person, or so they say. Their powers are from God. They must be. Everything that is supernatural is from God. Isn't it?

43

Many of the people who go to the old non-English church up in the hills past our house also have abilities. During the services people fall into trances while the spirit is telling them special things. Sometimes they bark like dogs or growl, but you shouldn't let it scare you, my mother says. Just leave them on the floor where they have fallen. After the trance is over and the message from the spirit has been communicated, they will sit down in the pew next to you again.

Our people also have the ability to actually see angels and evil spirits. Grandmother saw one next to her bed last month. It was a bad angel, not a good one, she says. Some of the people in the church have seen special visions in the sky. Sometimes two or three or more people all see the same vision at the same time. Then they know for sure that it is from God.

"Our people are more spiritual than the Americans. We can see into the spirit world in ways they can't."

hite pillars. A long covered front porch. These are the only clues my mind is giving me. I'm reminded of my nightmare once again today as I look through Grandmother's old trunk up here in the attic. Each time, my nightmare is exactly the same: two white pillars in front of a long covered porch. Whenever my mind tries to paint me a picture of this house in my dreams, a knot forms in the middle of my stomach. Slowly the knot tightens and becomes a terrible pressure inside. I want to run. I want to hide. I don't recognize the house. I only recognize the anguish on the inside. In my nightmare I scream myself awake and lie panting in my bed.

I dreamed about the white-pillared house again last night. All through the day today I've seen its picture before my eyes. It's as though I'm looking at a picture-perfect postcard of some important place. Now, as I look through Grandmother's trunk, my mind begins to fill in the blank places, to connect the dots in my memory. I see in my mind a little three-year-old girl walking slowly up to the front door of the scary house. The door opens as a man's hand turns the doorknob above my head. I can feel my father's hand holding mine as he walks beside me. He stops and lifts me up from under my arms.

On either side of an aisle there are rows of folding chairs filled with people—black dresses, black hats, the sweet but old smell of flowers. I'm sitting on my father's lap. I see the shiny black box with vases of red flowers all around it.

The people in black are walking down the aisle in a slow, sad line, each one looking into the tall box. Now only my mother and father and some other people are left to look. My father reaches down to where I have been playing with my shoelaces on the floor between the rows of chairs. He lifts me up and holds me in his arms as we too walk toward the shiny black box.

There is a lady sleeping in the box on a satiny white pillow with ruffles around the edges. She's wearing Grandmother's black dress. Her hands are resting on top of one another. Like Grandmother's, her wispy hair is pulled back in a bun. But the face is not Grandmother's. It has the same cheeks, the same nose, the same lips, but it doesn't look like her. The skin is yellow, and she's too still and quiet to be Grandmother. Grandmother always has her eyes open. She is always looking at me when I come and stand beside her. But this lady does not seem to see me looking down at her now.

My father leans up against the black box. As he moves forward, he accidentally pinches part of my leg between his waist and the box. He is saying something in a very low, quiet voice.

"Come into her now . . . we receive all that you give. . . ."

There are many more words that I don't understand. My ears are listening to my father, and my eyes are looking at the lady in the box. She is so still. She is so white. I don't realize where my hand is being placed until I feel the wax-like skin under my fingers. My father presses my palm against her cheek as he seals the spiritual agreement.

I feel something. It's like a wind blowing through me. It's a wind from my grandmother. She has had something, someone, living in her who now comes to me. I can feel the movement as things enter me. I'm frightened by the feeling. It seems as though there's not enough room inside for me to breathe. I see no one with my eyes, but it feels as though someone is pushing in on my chest. Invisible things. Unseen ones.

No one has heard my father's commitment made on my behalf. At least no human being has heard. But there are ones who have heard—ones who are willing to work through me as they have worked through my grandmother. I am the new chosen one. I am to replace her. I receive all the powers that she had while she was the center of the powerful ones in our family line. Now I am the one who is to be the center, the one who is to take her place. Now the round-faced little girl will begin to live in the very middle of all the wickedness.

I don't understand, but for the first time I can sense the terror that the ones within me cause. They are not thoughts. They are not feelings. They are workers, workers for the black prince. I am the chosen one. I have taken my place in the family line. The ceremony, the vows my father takes for me as we stand beside the coffin have been completed.

My father still holds me in his arms but something very, very important has just happened. My life has been forever changed. At age three, I don't know the theology of what has just happened. But God knows. He sees it all. God knows that the enemy has begun something new in my life. But He—the Almighty God, Ruler of Light—also has a plan.

* * * * *

The Cheerios float like little inner tubes in my younger brother's cereal bowl. He plays with them with his spoon, pushing them under the surface of the milk. He's standing beside the table with one knee propped up on the torn plastic of the kitchen chair. His eyes never talk to my eyes at times like these. His mind is filled with his Cheerios. His ears are filled with his own soft humming. They do not want to hear my screams.

He shifts his weight and partly sits on the chair, one leg still standing. I understand. He is already a stone inside. He feels nothing. He has to do that. Somehow, I don't hate him. Somehow, I understand. Somehow, I wish I were a boy. Then none of this would be happening to me. His eyes have the same stare, the same deadness that I see in my mother's eyes. He is in another world—his inside world. In all the years that I am used by my father and the other men, my brother and I never once speak about it. Never once do we plot together to escape. Never once does he speak of helping me. Never once does he seem to see, to hear, to care.

My mother is in the same room as my brother. She is also trying to be somewhere else. She, like him, doesn't seem to notice, doesn't seem to care. I watch her sometimes during the pause when my father is waiting for me to give in, to confess, or whatever his broken mind is trying to get me to do. She's washing the dishes now with her back to me. After the last pot is scrubbed, she wrings the dishrag out and begins cleaning the kitchen counter.

As she turns sideways I cock my head to catch her eye. But her eye doesn't want to be caught. She lifts the teapot quietly and cleans under it. She knows to be quiet. My father doesn't like noise. He breaks into a fresh rage whenever her noise breaks the silence.

"Are you ready now?" he asks.

I don't answer. I only stare. I have too many answers. I can't choose. Which one will stop the hurt? Which answer will turn this crazy man who used to be my father away from his plans? I have many answers.

"_____ you!"

"I'll never give in!"

"Please don't hurt me anymore."

"I'm sorry."

All the possible answers come tumbling silently into my head. I can't decide on an answer, so I just stare. My silence causes his rage to flame up. After you're hurt for a while, your mind, your body doesn't care anymore. They just seem to fall asleep while you are awake, and the pain seems to go far away from where you are.

This is one of those times. My mind wanders and I drift away, floating up above the pain, above the crazy man, above the impossible questioning, above the smell of liquor. I like being here up on the ceiling. From here I can see but not feel. I can see pain but not cry. I stay up here until after it is all over.

The little girl down below me is strong inside. She hasn't given in. She knows that it makes no difference. He will do what he wants to her anyway whether she "learns to cooperate" or not. I don't want to be her again until it is safe, until he has gone. When I rejoin her, she will start all over again being the little blonde girl who doesn't remember what has happened just now. After my father is done teaching me a lesson, my brother and I go outside and play together. He plays with his toys, and I play with mine—in silence. We dig in the dirt with our green tractors and swing on the homemade wooden swing underneath the maple tree at the side of the house.

The little girl that has just faced the crazy man will not ask, "Why me?" She will pretend that nothing happened. She knows, after all, why it happened. She was bad again.

"It was all my fault. It was all my fault."

* * * * *

The man with the window in his shirt comes today. That's what I call him. He has a window in his shirt. He's one of the twelve men, friends of my father, who pays $2 for me to be his wife. He's a quiet man. He has soft hands, a soft voice. He would be nice except he always wants me the way the other men want me. His cheeks are getting tired of staying up close under his eyes. They sag down closer to his mouth than the other men's.

His hair looks tired too. It's a used-to-be-black color that takes on an old gray look now. It's all thinned out across the top, and he keeps it flipped up over the bare spot in the middle. When it gets tousled, it hangs down over his forehead in long, straight, greasy threads.

After he leaves my bedroom, the sweet smell of his aftershave stays behind. Sometimes my cat carefully sniffs my pillow with her nose to see who has been with me. Sometimes all the smells of all the aftershaves mix together in a confused sort of way. When we go to a store downtown and I pass the aftershave aisle, sometimes I get sick inside. My mind forgets that this time that smell doesn't have a bad man with it.

Don't be afraid. It'll be all right.

But the smell of the man with the window in his shirt will be coming soon. And with it, the man who is so quiet and so gentle. I wish I could like him, but I can't. I'm sad inside because he could be nice, but he is not. He could be safe, but he is not. He could make the rest of him be just as gentle as his eyes are, but he does not.

He doesn't come as often as Rudy or some of the other men do. He comes only when he is near our house, after his official visits at other people's homes are over. It's hard for me to see him when others are around. He is his kindest, softest, gentlest at those times. He touches the other people's arms, puts his hand on their shoulders or pats the tops of their hands as he holds it in a firm grasp of care and concern.

My eyes don't meet his eyes at those times. I just watch his hands as they get dangerously close to the other people. But the people don't seem afraid. They don't seem to think that he will hurt them. They don't seem to sense how terrified I am for them. They don't know.

Don't be afraid. It'll be all right.

I see the man with the window in his shirt on another day of the week, too . . . Sunday. As I sit on the hard wooden pew, my eyes focus on that little window just as they do when he is hurting me. His tall black shirt collar makes a complete circle around his neck except for the little white square window in the very middle. He doesn't wear his pastor suit every day, only on the days when he is being official. After he comes to leave the smell of his aftershave on my pillow, he visits the sick in the hospital, and he tells us about God as he stands looking out over his congregation.

The man with the window in his shirt is one of the men I hate the most. He could be nice, but he isn't. He could take me away from all this terribleness, but he doesn't. He adds his own part to the pain. For a tiny minute, as his soft hands carefully brush my long hair out of my face and up behind my ear, I wish I belonged to his gentle side. I wish he would always take care of me. The softness is confusing. But as quickly as my wish settles in on me, it is rudely pushed out of the way by the hatred that wells up inside me. For the first three or four times he comes to me, the man with the window in his shirt whispers the same prayer after it's all over: "God, forgive me."

51

No one hears his guilty words as I lie with my ear close to his lips. No one except me and God. Every time he speaks his words of confession, I silently speak my words of revenge.

Make him burn in hell!

The violence that wells up inside me surprises even me. My teeth close tightly together so that the viciousness that comes with these words doesn't rush out and betray me. I know there is a hell. This man with the window in his shirt has taught us so. He's often read the verses from his big black Bible that make it very clear.

Wicked people go there. Mean people. Those who mock God. People like the man with the window in his shirt. He will be there someday himself, I tell myself. I've heard about forgiveness from this man's own lips as I sit in the pew in church. But as I lie here, I ask God to make this time be different.

Just this once, God, make him pay for hurting me.

Don't be afraid. It'll be all right.

"Just pick one, Laura." The rest of the students in my fourth grade class are getting tired of waiting. The teacher is a little more patient. But you can tell that she is ready to go on to Tommy. Then he can pick a colored sheet of construction paper from those fanned out in her hand. There are soft-looking pinks and hard-looking purples and hardly colored beiges.

It should be an easy thing to choose. But not for me. As the teacher stands beside my desk and holds out the choices, my mind seems to lock shut. It refuses to choose. First, it got confused; now it's staring at the wall inside my head, saying nothing, refusing to decide.

"How about pink? Pink would work nicely."

Mrs. Bryan is getting flustered with me. I nod and pull out the pink-edged one from the colorful papers in her hand. Why can't I choose? My mind seems suddenly to panic, to freeze, to go numb. It's not any good at deciding. Sometimes even the simplest choices make it stop moving, stop thinking altogether. It's stuck. The more people on the outside try to push it into a decision, the more it stands completely still and silent.

The same thing happens when people ask me questions. They think I am stupid when I can't answer them right away. They seem to think that if they keep asking with the same words over and over again, I will finally understand what they mean and give them an answer. But I do understand their words. It's just that my mind gets stuck. It's the same as trying to choose. The more they ask, the more the pressure and confusion inside builds.

Too fast.

Too fast.

They are going too fast.

It seems as though my mind keeps things in order inside by going just the right speed. It sees and thinks and decides. But when I have to choose, or people are waiting for my answer, it seems as though a whirlwind swirls through my mind, and everything goes too fast for it. I can feel the terror, the confusion, building. Then my mind just gets stuck. It does that a lot at home too.

"Why did you do it?"

My father's question is in our language, so I understand him very clearly. I can hear him clearly because he's shouting. I understand, but I have no answer.

"Why did you do it?"

His thumb and fingers pinch the top of each of my arms. His face is red. His eyes are hateful. His clenched teeth try to be a gate to keep back his angry words, but they are spoken anyway. My head turns in the opposite direction of the slaps it gets in between the questions. I don't have an answer. I don't know what he is talking about. He is in one of his wild rages again. He gets so filled with anger that sometimes his words don't come out in sentences. They are only a jumble of parts of words or sounds that mean nothing.

I don't know to ask him what he means. I know not to try to speak. If I do, he won't hear me. It is as though when his mind rages his ears become deaf. He doesn't even seem to know what is going on around him when the rage has him. He shakes me with both of his strong hands. My mind is stuck. My mouth refuses to let him know that I have heard his question. It's silent.

At first, as he begins his rage, I'm trembling on the inside. The craziness in his eyes always means that his mind is ready to receive the darkness, ready to let it take control. It will not be long. At first I have room only for terror inside. But now I'm singing inside. Singing happy tunes, wordless tunes—singing as though my sanity depended on it. My inner singing drowns out his voice.

It seems that after awhile I have to read his lips to tell what he is saying. I hear nothing but my calming voice inside singing. Everything outside of me is black and dark. My singing makes the inside part full of bright yellows and gentle blues. Sometimes my head bumps up against the wall behind me as he swings his fist. Then I don't have to see his face anymore. All is black. I wake up and look up from the floor. He is usually gone by then.

But this time he has not gone away. My eyes are looking out through smaller-than-usual openings. The throbbing in the back of my head where it found the wall is making it hard to see, hard to focus. But I can see her. She is tied with the same white clothesline rope that he usually ties me with. My eyes wish they were still seeing only black. The darkness has all of him now. His eyes are not his own. He has been hurting her. He keeps on hurting her. My eyes drop for a moment to the floor, refusing to look. But then I look up and watch.

It doesn't matter.

It doesn't hurt anymore inside.

I have already died inside.

I am already a stone inside.

I watch as though I was like one of the pieces of furniture that is witnessing these atrocities. I have no tears. My mind tells me that this is my mother, that I want to run to her, to untie her, to escape with her. But that is only my mind talking. In the places where there used to be feelings to agree with the words of my mind, there is only silence.

I am already a stone inside.

In an instant he turns toward me. Like a lion that is disturbed and turns away from the deer he is dismembering, my father notices that I am here again. He faces me suddenly and includes me in the horror.

"Come here! Come here!"

It's not him alone who speaks to me. It's the wickedness he has welcomed inside that now hisses at me through his lips. I don't move. I only stare into the murderous eyes. I'm not afraid. When there is too much fear, you can't feel it anymore. I am past fear.

I am already a stone inside.

"Come here, I said!" My father punctuates his command to me by thrusting his fist, full force, into my mother's stomach. I don't move. I say nothing. It becomes a game now for him. I can hear the thuds and moans as he is trying to prove that I will have to obey him in the end. I don't move. I don't come here. I know what he will have me do when I get there. If my hands will not do the sadistic things to her that he wills, his massive hands will hold them in his and use them as mute instruments of his wickedness. I do not move, and the beating continues.

My mother can't turn in my direction, but she is speaking to me. She uses the f-word that I hardly ever hear her use. She finishes her curse at me by screaming, "I hate you! I hate you! I hope you die. I'll kill you myself."

As she spits out her hateful words, the tearing inside of me begins again.

I cannot choose.

I cannot decide what to do.

My mind is stuck.

Impossible choices.

I cannot make my mind think.

I cannot pick the right answer.

There is no right answer.

Only my father's craziness.

I choose not to remember how long the torture goes on. I will make my hand circle around the farmer lady on the bedroom wallpaper again tonight. I will whisper to my cat as he snuggles up close to me in my bed, his loud motor running. I will tell Jesus.

Hold me, Jesus. Hold me.

And He does.

* * * * *

"Sure have had lots of rain, haven't we? We didn't get all our hay in before that last storm. Came up so quick."

My father passes the time with the other farmers in the congregation of our little church down in the valley. Most, like us, speak two languages—one at home with the older relatives and another with the English speakers at church or at school. Most, like my father, have only a fifth grade education. Most are hard workers. Most don't know.

The little white church has been standing here since before the turn of the century. Its worn wooden floors and dark wooden benches creak when you put your weight on them. There's that long ago, old smell that buildings get when the dampness mixes with the dust. The glass in the small window panes has sagged, and the bottom part of each distorts what you see through them. The wood-burning stove has long since been replaced by a modern furnace. It hums loudly from somewhere beneath the ornate black wrought-iron registers in the floor. Red velvet curtains frame the wooden cross behind the podium.

The large Sunday school room at the back of the sanctuary is divided into tiny cubicles by curtains on wire rings. Each room has just enough space for a table and a few chairs. During the summer, if the classes get too big, they move out into the three-sided shed behind the church. It was once a stable for keeping the horses during the services, but the children don't seem to mind the wooden benches and the dirt floor. The outhouse further back is full of wasp nests. You only use it if you have to.

"How 'bout you? All your hay in?"

I listen to my father talking to the neighbor man. This time they choose English as they talk with each other. This is an English church. We don't really fit in here, but we come anyway. It's the closest church to our farm. The word "Fundamental" is not printed with the other words over the front doors, but that's what kind of church it is. The Bible is preached and a personal relationship with Christ is taught. People try their best to resist sin. No dancing, no smoking, no swearing, no movies. The numbers are down now from fifty-four to thirty regular attenders. Maybe it's the new pastor, some think.

"No, can't say that I've heard that before."

My father likes to talk about safe things.

Nice things.

Things you can agree on.

The weather.

The crops.

The icy roads.

The church people like him. He smiles a lot and looks interested in the conversations. Sometimes he flirts in an acceptable way with the teenage girls and makes them giggle and blush. He's taught Sunday school before and recently has been chosen as the new Sunday school superintendent. He is also a deacon. Sometimes the pastor asks him to pray out loud during the prayer part of the service.

"Our heavenly Father . . ."

I try not to listen as his voice pauses for emphasis at all the right dramatic places. Church fits into Part A of my life: the normal part.

"We thank Thee that Thou hast . . ."

I watch a sleepy, half-drunk fly trying to stagger up the glass on the window to my left. He pauses every few steps, unsure of himself.

"For all our many blessings, our homes, our families, our children . . ."

I glance up at Roger. He is watching the fly too. Our eyes meet. I smile. Roger is nice. He's one year older than I am and an American, but he's nice.

I turn for a minute to watch my father as he stands and prays. His bloated stomach sags over his brown belt. He reminds me of a fat pumpkin with two posts for legs. His suit coat tries its best to fit him. The last time it really fit was several years and many pounds ago. The button in the middle holds everything together, or tries. My father only wears his suit to church and to funerals, so there's really no need to go to the expense of buying a new one.

The fly on the window has been joined by another. They're having a slow motion race to the top of the pane.

I like church.

I like to pretend.

I like to be happy and smile.

At church my father puts his arm across my shoulders as I sit next to him in the pew. He likes to touch me a lot. He smiles at me and calls me "baby doll" when others are listening. He has his Sunday smell of Old Spice aftershave on. He acts nice. I am safe at church. Church is one of the Part A places in my life. No one knows the Part B. When I am here, I pretend not to know either. It's nicer that way. Part B seems a long way off, like there is no Part B.

I must have made it up.

Maybe I dreamt it.

Maybe.

Maybe not.

'm having trouble with my mind. It wants to remind me. But I'm telling my remembering part not to come in. No room. I lock the door to my mind and tell it not to come in. When I shut the door to my mind, my thoughts try to push in at the windows.

Go away!

Leave me alone!

My mind does what it wants, pictures what it wants, remembers what it wants. It's like a determined preschooler trying to break free, insisting on going where she wants to go. I'm having trouble with my mind. It wants to remind me. I will distract my mind.

Hi, Mr. Ant. Where are you going?

Let's see now, how many legs do you have?

Do ants have eyes?

I will comfort my mind.

Shh . . . shh. . . .

Don't be afraid.

It'll be all right.

Rock, rock; rock, rock.

See-saw; see-saw.

Rock, rock; rock, rock.

Humming always helps.

Long, calming, soft sounds bring a numbing inside.

Don't be afraid. It'll be all right.

I say it once again out loud just to convince myself.

I'm having trouble with my mind. It wants to remind me. Sometimes it's easy to forget. I can make the pain go away with my mind. I take it from where it is and move it far away from me. So, when my long sleeves cover the fresh marks on my arms, my mind gets tricked into forgetting. My body nods in agreement. Nothing happened. Nothing. I don't remember anything. I don't feel anything, it innocently reports. It's harder if I see the burns or welts or bruises. Then the helium-filled balloon of my memory pops up to the surface. The battle starts all over again—the battle to forget.

Today, I'm having trouble with my mind.

It wants to remind me.

The volcano inside erupts in a fiery explosion. Some kind of terror inside makes me race out of the house, down past the barns and out into the woods. I run and run as though the scar-makers still have me. I run full out until I can't run anymore. I try to catch my breath. My heavy breathing frightens me. It's like the sound of his breathing, so close, so warm, next to my ear.

My arms and legs are jumping uncontrollably. My eyes dart terrified from side to side, blurring the trees and fallen leaves. My stomach chooses this time to empty itself. My teeth begin to click noisily together ignoring my attempts to keep them still. The hammering in my chest keeps pounding faster and faster until it catches up with itself and stumbles on ahead. A snapped twig from a squirrel's jump makes me huddle up against the rough bark of the tree behind me.

Oh, God. Oh, God. Help me. Help me.

The dam inside has burst. The restraining walls that keep back the memories have crumbled. The rush of terror and remembering comes gushing forward, drowning all other thoughts.

The burning!

The burning!

I remember the burning.

My mind paints a vivid picture of what happened earlier today. They're not happy with me. I have displeased Rudy again by biting him as he crushed me under his own weight. They will teach me. I'll never do that again, they say.

One holds me from behind, the other stretches out my arm. My teeth lock. I will not scream. I will not scream. Even if they laugh, I will not scream. My eyes carry my mind into the neatly patterned jets of fire circling the burner. Blue and white. The flame flickers as his breath blows down on it. I don't look at the knife. It is my enemy; I hate it.

Once upon a time there was a princess called Snow White . . . and seven dwarfs. . . . All of my usual helpers inside, my mental games, are not enough to block out the burning. My nausea wells up from deep inside, and I swallow deliberately to control it. My eyes have left the flame now, as has the knife. I am not focusing anywhere in particular. It's as though I am once again somewhere above myself, a safe distance from the pain.

I can hear and smell when the knife arrives. Oh, God. It's a sound and a smell like no other. It will be with me tonight as I circle the farmer lady on the wallpaper, trying to forget. It will suddenly rush to my nose and ears tomorrow as my father casually flicks his lighter and brings it up to his cigarette. It will be with me months from now. My father will stare at me with icy eyes and remind me of this day by clicking his shiny lighter open and shut, open and shut.

Our secret.

Our code.

His message is clear.

As I am learning my lesson by the stove no screams escape. Other than my faint moans no sounds come out of my mouth. My jaws are still locked. I have the key. I will not let them hear me scream. They will not win. They will never win!

Hang on to me, Jesus.

* * * * *

Please, God, take me away. Don't leave me here with all these crazy people. They'll kill me soon by accident if I stay here much longer.

I'm in my room now, snuggled up close to my cat. I'm sad, but I'm also busy forgetting. I rock from side to side as best I can as I lie here in the dark. It has been the kind of day I have two or three times a week; the kind of day that is full of dirty memories, hurting memories, terrifying memories. I wish I weren't a girl. I wish I were a strong, tall man. Then I could fight with the men when they come to take me. Then I could get in the car and drive away to a new place, a sane place. I wish I could get away from here before morning.

As I lie here in my bed with my cat beside me, I remember my father's words spoken not many hours ago. He's been in a rage again tonight. He has let the darkness take over. His eyes are not his own. He's been teaching me a lesson again. His breath smells of beer as he pulls my face close to his.

"You told, didn't you?"

He accuses me of something that I have not done, that I could never do. I have too colorful a picture in my mind of the consequences.

"What did I tell you I'd do if you ever told?"

He questions me, but I know he doesn't want an answer. It makes no difference if I answer him or not. He is just as crazy either way. His eyes seem to boil over with hate as he pulls my face inches from his own. He whispers his threat so softly that my own ears barely make out his words. "In the morning, I'll peel your skin off with a knife. Do you understand? I'll teach you what happens when you tell. Now, get out of here!"

He punctuates his last sentence by knocking me across the dining room. As I pick myself up and walk slowly off to my room, my voice is silent, but my mind is screaming. His words have reminded me of his promise of what he will do to me if I ever tell. I'm glad that my cat is already safe in my bed when I get to my room. Sometimes she is not so safe with a crazy man in the house. But she's unhurt tonight. I change into my pajamas quickly and bury my face in her comforting fur.

As I rock my head and shoulders from side to side, I try to forget. But somehow, tonight, I can't forget. The screaming inside has become so loud and so bone-chilling that I can't sleep. I try to erase the day, the pain, the sound of my father's threatening voice by circling the farmer lady on the wallpaper. But this time it doesn't work.

After the house is quiet and everyone has gone to bed, I hear the slow, rhythmic breathing from my father's room that tells me that I can let my stomach unknot now. But it won't relax. The picture of what he will do in the morning is too vivid, too hellish. It will not go away. As I lie in the darkness, I hear a thought in my head. It's as though God is speaking to me.

I will help you. I will rescue you. I will send an angel to get you tonight. He will bring you to me. You must stay by the stove. He will come to you there.

I listen to the calm, low voice inside. Hope. An angel is coming to take me away. I will be gone before my father's threat for the morning can happen. I do not question where the voice is from. It must be from God. He is coming to help me, to take me away.

My bare feet are surprised by the cold wooden floor of my bedroom as I get out of bed. What about my cat? Who will take care of my cat? What should I do? Please tell me what to do.

"You must stay by the stove. The angel will come to get you there."

The stove is at the end of the counters in the kitchen, beside the refrigerator. There's no wall between the dining room and the kitchen, so one side of the old white stove acts as a divider between the two small rooms.

I'm waiting by the stove as the angel said. I've thought to put my slippers on, and I sit cross-legged by the side of the stove. He is coming for me. He will take me away. I won't have to live in this crazy house anymore. An angel is coming. I will go to be with God.

I don't know what time it is as I obey the voice's command and come to the stove. I don't know what time it is as I wait for the promised angel. I don't know what time it is as I get tired and lean my head and shoulder up against the smooth, chilled surface of the silent stove. I have to stay awake, or I may miss him when he comes. I lean against the cold metal and begin to make circles with my fingers on the slippery surface next to me.

He must be coming soon.

He must be.

I must wait by the stove.

Eight

He will come.

I don't know what time it is as I wake from my sleep. At first I don't remember where I am. But then I hear my mother in the bathroom at the other end of the house. I recognize the cold, white surface I am resting against. I remember everything. I remember everything, and I die a little more inside.

He hasn't come.

He hasn't sent an angel.

He hasn't taken me away.

My eyes are used to holding in my tears. But they can't hold them all in as I notice that the morning dawn is beginning outside the kitchen window. I shut my eyes tightly and try to keep them back. But it's no use. Tears escape through the corners of my eyes.

Despair.

Sadness.

Emptiness.

I make my way to my bedroom before my mother notices me. My cat is already taking her morning washup. She stretches her front legs out in front of her as I climb into the bed beside her. And in my head I hear the voice again. It is the same one that talked to me last night. It is the one who told me to wait by the stove. It is the one who filled me with hope. But now it has a different face on. It is mocking me. It is laughing at me in a wicked sneer. It is of the darkness. It was not God at all. It was the other god, the one I hate. It is the one who likes to rob me of my hope.

I'm startled from those thoughts by the sound of my father's creaking bed. He's getting up. I can hear his feet slide between his steps as he walks with a hangover. My stomach clenches into a knot as I await his promised torture.

But it doesn't happen. He doesn't come. I hear the sounds that tell me that he's getting ready for work. I hear the click as he sets his coffee cup down on the tabletop one last time.

As I hear the car in the driveway outside my window cough to a start, I know for sure that he is not coming for me. He has forgotten. His eyes are his own now. The darkness is gone for awhile. He is once again in Part A. My terror is over for now, but I am not the same. Somewhere deep down on the inside, there is less of me that wants to hang on. There is less of me that wants to keep going.

Please, God, hang on to me. I hurt inside.

W hy are you doing that?

Because I have to.

No, you don't.

Yes, I do.

I have heard the voices, the conversations, inside my head since before I started kindergarten. There are more than one. Sometimes I can hear them arguing among themselves. It's like listening to two friends talking together while I stand off to the side and watch. I see them as more than voices. They are like people inside of me, part of me, yet separate.

Some of the voices are mad. I can picture them clenching their fists and gritting their teeth as their anger simmers under their words. Some are very sad and seem to fill me with a grayness that seeps over all of me. They have a tiredness around them that tugs at me inside. Some are terrified. They are the screamers. I have heard that screaming from somewhere in the back, deep part of my mind for as long as I can remember. It's like having a radio playing somewhere off in the background. It's not on loud enough to come to the front of my mind, but neither is it soft enough to go unnoticed.

The screaming is not the short, weak squeals of people who are mad that they didn't get their way. It is the heart-wrenching, top-of-the-lungs screaming of a tortured, wild-eyed soul. I can see a vivid picture of the screaming one. She sits in a dark room all by herself, somewhere deep inside me. In her rage her scraggly hair has fallen forward over her sweaty face. But she doesn't seem to notice. She is in anguish. She is filled with terror. She is crazy. All she does is scream and scream and scream and scream.

I don't always see her in my mind's eye, but I can always hear her screams. They are the kind from horror movies where the girl has just turned suddenly and come face to face with the monster. She opens her eyes wide in terror and screams as loud and as long as her lungs will let her.

The screaming inside my head is also mixed with a rage, a rattling-at-the-bars-of-the-cage sort of rage that goes on and on. Her nonstop terror makes it hard for me to concentrate. When I'm sitting at my desk at school, I hear her screaming. When I'm coloring pictures in my Sunday school class, I hear her screaming. When I'm working out in the fields with my father and my brother, I hear her screaming. When I'm lying awake in bed and all else is quiet, I can hear her screaming the loudest.

She never stops. Her anguish goes on and on.

I'm afraid of the screamer inside. She is insane. I can tell by the way she looks. I can tell by the wild look in her eyes. And, if I listen very closely, I can tell by the babbling she sometimes breaks into. I'm afraid of her. So are the other voices inside.

Who are these voices?

I call them "my sisters." They have been with me as long as I can recall. I don't ask myself how they got there or if other people have sisters inside. I believe that everyone must, like me, be able to carry on two conversations at once—one on the outside with other people and one on the inside with the voices. They're like friends to me. They're also part of me. I don't try to explain where they begin and I end. It doesn't bother me that they are part of my mind yet somehow separate from it. But somewhere within there is the knowing that they are me or at least part of me.

I don't think of myself as being crazy. I don't connect the splitting up on the inside with the horror that I have to live through each week at the farm when Part B—the insane part—comes. I only know that when I'm at the end of hanging on, when the pain is too big or the terror is smothering me, it feels like my mind blows up. When Rudy is playing his sadistic games, I feel myself escaping the physical pain by tearing away inside and floating to the ceiling. I can watch from there at a safe distance. I see, but I don't feel.

When my mother is being burned or tortured in some other way in front of my eyes, I feel the bubble of air inside my chest becoming two bubbles of air. Then I begin watching the torture as though I were sitting in the second row from the front in a movie theater. I see the horrible play being performed, but I am not part of it. There's someone else now sitting in that front-row seat. I'm looking over her shoulder, from behind, watching her watching the horrible events as they unfold before her eyes.

The front-row seat is the place where you feel the pain. Here in the second row I see and think of what is happening, but I don't feel it. I can now look on and be a stone inside. It doesn't matter anymore to me. I've seen things that no one's eyes are able to see. I've had to make choices—impossible choices—that no one is able to make. I've lived with an anguish that's too big for a little girl to carry. I've touched spiritual darkness and been surrounded by it. I've lived a life that no one is able to survive without the help of the Creator God.

My God, the God of the Bible, keeps me alive. He helps me to keep going. He gives my mind a chance to stay alive and sane by letting it divide somehow. But the will of the Creator is that someday the parts of my mind will again become one. Someday the image will once again come into sharp focus. Someday I will be reminded by my Father that I don't need to be afraid.

It will be all right.

* * * * *

"When we all get to heav-en, what a day of re-joic-ing that will be . . ."

Everyone sings loudly even if they can't carry a tune very well. The pastor's wife sings solos sometimes. She is a stout but kind lady. I like her. She has soft hands and twinkling, dark eyes. Her wide smile fills up her face and makes her eyes move up a little to give her mouth more room. I dream about her and the pastor almost every night before I go to sleep. I say dream, but it happens while I am awake. For two or three hours each night I lie awake and listen for the footsteps. It helps if I dream about my new home with the new pastor and his wife. He is tall and thin, and his glasses encircle gentle brown eyes.

I dream I belong to them. I dream I live at their green house next to the church. I dream that they love me and take care of me and say things like, "Are you sure you'll be warm enough in that coat?" or, "Did you get enough to eat?" I dream my life is happy. I dream my life always stays the same. But as I begin to doze off each night, my mind always puts a scary ending on my happy dream. One day the pastor and his wife can't find me. I am outside their house in the front yard, trapped in a wooden box. They call and call, but they don't realize I'm locked away in the box. I scream and scream, but somehow they can't hear me. Sometimes I scream out loud and wake myself up.

I feel so alone.

I feel so sad.

No one at church knows. Except maybe old Mrs. Carter. I walk to the church by myself on Wednesdays. Sometimes my mother comes too. My father doesn't like to go to prayer meeting, so mostly I go there alone.

Once last winter my wandering mind was stopped short as I heard Mrs. Carter unexpectedly say a short, simple prayer:

Lord, keep Laura from the dangers around her. Keep her safe, dear Lord.

Such a brief request. Does she really know how much it was needed? Does she know about Part B? I wish somebody knew. I have to tell someone. I'm afraid my father and his friends will kill me. I'll tell Mrs. Frank, I decide.

She will listen.

She will believe me.

She will help.

Mr. and Mrs. Frank go to our church. They have eight children. Maybe they will want one more. She's cooking in the kitchen when I knock. She wipes her hands on the blue-checkered dish towel and smiles as she swings open the wooden screen door for me. Her face is red. There are lots of tiny beads of sweat on her forehead. She blots them with her towel before she invites me to sit down. The screen door makes me jump as the metal spring loudly snaps it shut.

I smell apple pies baking as I cross the cracked linoleum of the large farm kitchen. I pull out one of the tall wooden chairs and sit by the table. Mrs. Frank offers me some lemonade and tells me that Debbie is out behind the barn helping her dad. Debbie is my age. We are in the same Sunday school class.

You don't have to worry about things to talk about with Mrs. Frank. She's a jolly, talkative person. Sometimes she fills in both parts of the conversation all by herself. We talk some about small things. I try to silence the terror inside at least long enough to tell her.

"I look at your family, and it seems so nice," I say.

I have rehearsed over and over again how I am going to start.

"Sometimes it makes me wish I were a part of this family," I say.

Even without turning away from peeling her apples at the sink, Mrs. Frank shatters any hope I have.

"Don't be silly," she says with an embarrassed laugh. "How could you say that? Your father is such a wonderful man and such a strong Christian too. How could you ever say such a thing?" She adds another little laugh as her tone of voice announces the end of the discussion.

I had imagined it going so differently. I hadn't even had a chance to roll up my long sleeves and show her the marks on my arms, the proof that he was not as wonderful a man as people at the church think he is.

Please. Please.

Don't laugh at me.

Don't make fun of me.

Please believe me.

Please don't shut me out.

Please, please, don't take away my hope.

The words cascade through my head, but none reach my mouth. There are degrees of deadness. I come to a new level as I smell her pies and listen to her chattering. Her mocking reproach has driven me further inside myself, closer to the belief that mocks me from within: You'll never escape. You'll never get away. Nobody cares. Nobody.

Please, God, hang on to me.

My mother is confused. She doesn't know what she should do. I can hear her footsteps. I know her walk. She isn't as heavy as my father is. She walks lighter. I can hear her as she slides open the big wooden door of the barn. She closes it after her as if to keep what has happened inside a secret. No one must know. No one must see what her husband's craziness has done to her ten-year-old daughter.

She's in the front part of the barn now. I can hear as she walks past the farm equipment and opens the creaking door to the cow stalls. She must be looking for me. She's not sure what has happened to me since she saw both my father and me enter the barn this morning. He has long since returned to the fields to work. He has gone in for dinner. It's beginning to get dark. Did she ask him? Did she demand to know what he has done to her little girl? Did she threaten to call the police? Did she storm out of the house, looking frantically for me?

No. Instead she waits until after dinner, until after he has once again returned to the fields. She never interferes. She never argues with him. She lets him discipline her little girl as he sees fit.

I've long since lost the feeling in my arms. As they stretch over my head, the rope digs deeply into my wrists. But I can't feel it. The terrible pain in my shoulders and back has long since been replaced by a cool comforting numbness. The hours since he suspended me here have gone by slowly: one hour, three, five, seven. I have no way of knowing the time. At first there is too much pain. After that, I am too distracted.

I've been watching the little shafts of bright light. They shine through the knothole in the old wood of the barn walls and make spotlights for the hay dust to dance in. The dust is shiny like yellow gold. It is drifting like a dream in the long columns of light that reach all the way to the barn floor.

It's a hot sticky evening in August. The rasping sound that comes when I breathe is not from what happened before I was left up here. No, it's from the hay dust. I have asthma. The whistling sound coming up from my lungs becomes like a friend to me, like a second person being put here by my father "to learn her lesson."

This part of the barn has a metal roof. Earlier in the day, as the sun beat down on it, the little rivers of sweat trickled down my face. But it's cooler now. The air smells the way it does before a rain shower.

There is an annoying strand of long blonde hair hanging down in the wrong place, right over my left eye. The sweat has cemented it to my forehead, and nothing I do can convince it to move. Only my soft singing has helped to distract me and kept me from claustrophobia.

I wish my hands were free.

They could help me.

I wish someone would help me.

Maybe my mother will help me.

She's coming now. I can hear her getting closer, almost at the doorway between the two parts of the barn. My back is to the door, so I can't see her face as she enters and stops in silence.

Silent.

That has always been a good word to describe my mother. Whatever kinds of fears, whatever wounds from her own past, whatever has happened to her that makes it so easy for her to have her sister inside take over—all of that has accomplished one thing. It has made her silent. She's silent now as she looks up at her daughter. I don't know what she is thinking. I can't see her face. She makes no gasp, no sound. Maybe she's deciding, deciding if she will defy him and interfere with his discipline. Maybe she's hoping that like other times he will come in the house, begin drinking and forget that he is teaching me a lesson.

She moves a little bit forward. I can see her skirt out of the corner of my eye. She's standing still again. I am embarrassed. I don't want her to see me like this. I wish all of my clothes were on. She probably hates me for making him so mad that he had to do this to me.

She is silent.

I am silent too.

But inside, I'm begging. I'm begging her to help me. I'm begging her to cut me down. I'm begging her to free my hands so that I can brush the hair out of my face.

Silently I'm begging.

The rope goes up over my head to the overhanging beam that juts out from the main part of the barn. From there it goes down to the place where it's tied fast to a wooden railing. My mother moves past me. I can't see her out of the corner of my eye anymore. I hear her as she works the knot out of the thick rope and lets me down from over her head. The rope scrapes the railing as I'm being lowered. My eyes tell me that my legs have touched the dusty barn floor, but they can't feel it. They collapse under me. I've fallen forward, lying on the side of my face with my hands still tied together at the wrist.

I make my eyes look somewhere else as she kneels and unties my hands. Somehow I don't want to look into her eyes. If I do, that would be saying, "Look what he's done to me." I don't want to say that. I want to pretend that this has never happened, just as I do with all the other awful things he does to me.

She doesn't want to look into my eyes either. She stands up after she has untied me and, without a word, she leaves. I can hear her walking lightly across the worn barn floor. I can hear her as she slides open the big wooden front door of the barn. She closes it after her as if to keep what has happened there a secret. No one must know. No one must see what her husband's craziness has done to her daughter.

I don't move for a long time even after the rope is loosened. My arms, my wrists, tell me that they're still bound.

As the circulation begins to come back into my arms, my legs, my shoulders, the pain begins again. Only this time it seems worse. As I wait to be able to walk, I rock silently back and forth to comfort myself.

> Jesus loves me, this I know
> for the Bible tells me so. . . .
>   I'm glad He loves me.
>   I'm glad somebody loves me.

he holocaust.
The night of terror.
The Nazis.

A kind of strange quietness settles over my class as the history teacher discusses the unspeakable. The black-and-white pictures in our textbook show the shriveled bodies of those who used to be people.

The other kids seem to have a kind of fascination as they quietly study the pictures. The easily seen rib cages; the arm bones with skeleton hands attached to the ends; the filth; the stubble on the sunken faces. No part of the tragedy goes unnoticed. But for me, it's the eyes. They stare through the barbed wire as though they're too tired to blink.

The eyes.

They seem too big, too round for the rest of the face. They have a way of speaking without talking to those of us who know, who have seen some of what they have seen. The people are still able to stand or lie down. Somehow they have hung on and are still breathing. But their eyes give them away.

They are not alive.

They are already dead.

They have seen too much.

They have heard too many screams.

They have held on and held on until there was no more energy or will to bother anymore. Their whole story, from beginning to end, is recorded in their eyes.

I look at the picture of the little boy standing alone next to the barbed wire fence that shuts him in. Behind him, tall piles of corpses with tangled arms and legs silently rage against all that he has had to endure. He still has on his tattered, long-sleeved shirt and his knee-length pants. His flat-topped cap with the button in the middle is cocked to one side. His hands and face are dirty, and his hair sticks out in a tangle from under his cap.

I study his eyes.

They give him away.

He is already dead.

In them I can see my own eyes reflected.

When you've seen or felt torture, you don't worry about comparing someone else's anguish with your own personal holocaust. Torture is torture. Atrocities are atrocities. They all come from the same place. They all have the same fingerprints of the prince of darkness on them. They all have come from the inhuman mind of one with the ability to imagine unimaginable torments.

The little boy, and what is left of the other people in the pictures, seem to be glad that I understand, at least a little. I can never realize how deep the horror is that they hold inside. My life can never match the nonstop terror that they have had to live with. But I can understand at least a little. I can see something in their eyes that the other kids in my class miss. I can see the numbness that comes after the mind and the feelings have run out of energy to stay sane. At those times there's another type of sanity that takes over. When everything in your world is insane, inhuman, beyond explanation, you make your own sanity, your own world. The little boy in the photograph has made his own world within. He has had to. If he didn't, he would already have gone crazy.

But there's a difference between us. He has no sane part to his world. It's all inhumane, all crazy. I have the crazy part, but I also have a sane, normal part. That's why my eyes don't give me away. I have a place for all the craziness inside my mind. I keep it there, far from my normal part. I can laugh and smile and talk to the other kids and work on my schoolwork. I can be normal. I can make myself forget about the torture. Most of the time.

Torture and abuse are very different things. Abuse happens when someone wants something and doesn't care what he has to do to the other person to get it. Getting what he wants is the most important thing. The hurt that comes to the other is an unimportant byproduct.

But torture is somehow different. Torture is systematic, a planned terror. It wants only to inflict pain. It wants only to destroy the other person. Torture enjoys the terror and pain it causes. The more pain, the more screaming there is, the more the torturer smiles. It has no purpose—except viciousness.

The little boy in the picture seems like someone I know somehow. He and I have both seen things that human eyes were never made to see. He and I have both known the hideousness of watching and hearing others being tortured. The eyes of the Nazis reflect the same being that controls my father when he changes into his brutal side. The little boy in the picture and I have faced the same source of evil.

My memories of torture are in the farthest places, the deepest wells inside my mind. Sometimes I peer down over the rim into the darkness. I take a look at the photos my mind has taken. I see the little girl with blonde hair watching her toes as her bare feet tickle the strawberries around her. She rocks from side to side as her foot caresses the green leaves.

She's sitting on the ground at the edge of the field under the maple trees. Her bare legs crush the grass under them as she stretches them out in front of her. Her nose can smell the dampness of the woods behind her. She can smell the sweetness of the tiny wild berries that have popped up in the bare spots among the grass. Her face can feel the breath of wind that barely moves the bangs on her forehead.

She's trying hard. She's trying hard to fill her mind with the smell of the woods and the berries and the way the grass feels beneath her legs. She's trying hard. She's trying hard not to hear the sounds and see the things going on around her. She's trying not to hear the sounds of her father's irrational ranting. She's trying not to hear the sound of the farm tractor as he drives it past her back and forth, again and again, as she sits calmly among the strawberries.

She's trying not to learn what her father is trying to teach her. He is telling her that this is what happens when the little girl in the strawberries dares to disobey him. She's trying not to hear the sound of what is being dragged behind the tractor. She's trying not to see the dust that is stirred up. She refuses to see the rope that's pulled tight as the person tied to its end tries to run behind the moving tractor.

She doesn't see when her mother can't run fast enough to keep up with the wild man whose hand is on the steering wheel. She will not look as she is dragged past where the strawberries are tickling her daughter's feet. She tries not to look at the scrapes and cuts on her mother's arms and legs and the rawness on the side of her face after the insanity has passed.

She will have to tell lies again—lies about why her mother isn't feeling well enough to come to church on Sunday or why the little girl can't think well enough to take her math test at school on Monday. Her mind will still be filled with the dust and the strawberries and the woods and the torture she has been forced to watch. She has been told that this has all happened because she dared to disobey her father.

Yesterday, he had made it clear to her mother that the little blonde-haired girl was to wear the nice green dress when Rudy came this time to make her his wife. But the little girl insisted on wearing her other dress. In the back field her father showed her what her disobedience cost. It was her fault.

Oh, God! Oh, God!

I hate strawberries.

I hate grass.

I hate me.

* * * * *

My body is trying to tell me what my mind is trying to hide. My mind has won. All the circles I've traced with my finger around the farmer lady on the wallpaper have erased the truth, the reality of the first fourteen years of my life.

I'm seventeen now, and it's been three years since the abuse has ended. In a moment of bravery, and partly with the use of the psychic powers I have always had, I stand up to my father.

"If you ever touch me again, I'll kill you."

I hear the words hissing through my lips. Somewhere tangled up in them is a rage so deep that committing murder is a possibility.

With the end of the terror has come the end of my memories of the terror. I have chosen to forget. But my body is trying to tell me what my mind is trying to hide. I'm listening to Mozart's *Eine Kleine Nachtmusik* for my fine arts senior class. I lean forward and rub my forehead with my hand. I can make my finger trace the little ridge that goes all the way from the bone above my right eye, up through my forehead. Then the crack zigzags a little as it meanders across the right side of my skull and ends up somewhere above my right ear. I don't have such a crack on the other side of my forehead, only on the right side. I wonder why I don't have two. I don't remember when the crack first came.

My body is trying to tell me what my mind is trying to hide.

I also have to have an operation to repair the cartilage in my nose. I need the operation because somehow the soft tissue in my nose has been crushed in and is interfering with my breathing. I don't know how it got that way. I don't remember when it was damaged.

My body is trying to tell me what my mind is trying to hide.

There are other odd secrets too. Sometimes I can see a perfectly shaped imprint above and off to the right side of my rib cage. As I stand in front of the mirror drying myself, I look at the odd red mark. It's in the shape of a boot heel. It's most easily seen at those times like now after a hot shower when my skin takes on a translucent look. I don't know why it's there or when it got there.

My body is trying to tell me what my mind is trying to hide.

The small round scars—the one on the side of my face an inch or so in front of my ear and others on my stomach and on the inner part of my upper leg—they've always been there too. I've never asked how they got there. They just are there—round little circles the shape of the end of a cigarette. Why are they there? I never ask. I don't remember when the scar-makers put them there.

My body is trying to tell me what my mind is trying to hide.

My constant neck and shoulder pain is beginning to be a problem too. I have trouble in my physical education class. Both of my shoulders have become dislocated several times. Perhaps all the heavy lifting of the farm work I did when I was younger has weakened the muscles across my shoulders.

My body is trying to tell me what my mind is trying to hide.

When I go for X-rays at the chiropractor's, he tells me that they show that the corners of several of the vertebrae in my neck have been crushed. I stand beside him as together we inspect the negatives clipped to the light box. It's plain to see that what he says is true. I don't know how that happened. I don't remember when a blow or blows to my head were so severe that they crushed parts of the bones in my neck.

My body is trying to tell me what my mind is trying to hide.

* * * * *

As the commencement speaker talks, my fingers reach for the black tassel hanging down from my graduation cap. I roll the strands separately between my fingers and smile to myself. My grades have been excellent. I've had a good life so far.

Part A, the normal part, is all I know now.

Part B, the bizarre part, is long forgotten.

Not a fading memory, but an instant dramatic forgetting.

Not trying to be forgotten, but now entirely forgotten.

A mental eclipse.

I'm an expert at forgetting.

My graduation pictures show a girl with a quiet smile and sparkling eyes. I laugh easily. I'm a good listener, a good friend.

I'm an expert at forgetting.

But everything is not as it seems. The outward laughs and friendly smiles are contrasted with an inner unsettledness.

There's something wrong inside, but I don't know what it is. Somewhere deep within it seems that things are not as they should be. It's as though there's an empty, blank place in my mind. What is it? I don't want to know. It frightens me to think of it, to try to figure it out.

I'm an expert at forgetting.

I've had to be to survive.

God, what's happening? Help me.

The dorm floor here at my college is almost vacuumed now. Just a little more under my bed. Not much space here in a room designed for two students, now crowded with five.

My freshman year has been pretty nice so far. I work the night shift in the mailing room to make enough money to stay at school. But that's OK. I pour myself into my major and have kept very busy with my job and studies.

But something is beginning to happen. My mind is letting me know that there's a person, a being, a something within. I'm aware of a presence inside me.

I noticed it a few weeks after coming here to college. At first it seemed like a kind of movement inside. Not a physical sensation, but something else. But slowly, over the last few months, that vague feeling has turned into an awareness of a voice, a face, a dark presence within.

God, what's happening? Help me.

Now, as I vacuum, something strange is happening. Something, someone, the voice inside is enticing me to the window of our fourth-story dorm room. As desperately as a thirsty man begs for a drink of water, my mind is begging. It's begging me to shut off the vacuum, walk to the window, climb to the ledge, close my eyes and jump.

I'm terrified. Why? Why would I kill myself? Why would I do such a violent thing? The more I try to continue vacuuming, the more intense the craving for death grows within.

God, what's happening? Help me.

Sleep. Sleep. I'll go to sleep.

Maybe that will distract my mind, stop the terror.

My roommates will later tell me that they find me asleep when they return to the room. They try to wake me up, but the wild-eyed person looking up at them from the bed is not the Laura they know. I sit up in bed and stare at them with a chilling, other-world kind of look. They try to shake me awake, assuming that I'm dreaming. But they can't seem to get the real Laura back again.

This afternoon of vacuuming will be the beginning of a terrifying space of time in my life—a tormented four years—that is totally beyond my explanation. I'm suddenly filled with a lust for dying that makes no sense to my forgetting mind. Why would I want to kill myself? I don't have anything to be upset about, my Part A mind tells me. I've had a good life. I have a nice family. Things have always gone well.

God, what's happening? Help me.

It won't take long for the faculty and staff to become aware of my bizarre behavior. They will have to rescue me from balconies, from lakes, from the tops of high-rise buildings. I don't recall climbing onto the ledge. I only remember finding myself there, with worried friends pleading with me as they cautiously reach for me with outstretched arms.

God, what's happening? Help me.

Maybe I'm sleepwalking. I've done that since I was a child. I always run to the windows and scratch at the window screens with my fingernails, trying to escape. That nightmare has been with me for years. Maybe what I'm doing now in the day is like a nightmare. But why? I have no reason for this lust for death.

My friend Ruth had a reason. She didn't show up for school yesterday. The police found her with a bullet hole between her eyes. Ruth had a reason. She was caught in a trap of incest, of abuse, of confusion. She had a reason to take her own life. I don't. I've had a good life. I feel ashamed as I compare my happy life to Ruth's.

God, what's happening? Help me.

I've started carrying a long knife, hidden in my textbooks, to class. I don't know why. Perhaps it will provide an easy way out if I decide to end my life before the class ends. But someone has seen the end of the knife sticking out from the book under my chair. She spoke to the dean of women. I'm in her office now, being encouraged to go for counseling. I don't think I need counseling. I don't have problems like my friend Ruth. I've had a happy life. But why am I doing such bizarre things?

God, what's happening? Help me.

ELEVEN

"Why won't you look at me when you talk? It makes me feel like you're shutting me out."

When I first begin to see Dr. Blake, I go to his office five days a week. I'm in a crisis, the dean of women says.

I never look at him when we talk together. I can't. Something within me screams that I'm betraying everyone. But the people back on the farm don't have to worry. Their secrets are safe. I have no memories to tell this psychologist. I only speak of what's on the inside. I speak of the volcano. I speak of the murderous rage. I speak of the attempts to end the pain. I speak of the anguish. I speak of the fox's face.

Like a mask at a masquerade, the fox's face comes between me and what I'm looking at. It's as though the creature is close to my face, eye level, staring at me with burning eyes. He's inside my head. And with him comes a murderous blackness. It's been this way since I came to college. Now, in my second year, the concerned faculty has sent me here to Dr. Blake's office with hopes that I'll get help.

Maybe *he* can help me.

I run my fingers in a circle on the soft leather couch as I sit before this Christian psychologist. Maybe he can point me to God. Somewhere inside I know that God has the answer. Somewhere inside my hope for release from the insanity within has not yet quite been destroyed.

Maybe *he* can help me.

When I speak about talking to God, about trusting in Him to unravel the pieces, Dr. Blake seems disinterested. He never pursues that kind of subject. He always changes the topic. He doesn't seem to be close to God. So I talk about the farm. Part A. That's all I can remember. I talk about how we worked hard. I talk about my kind mother. I talk about my Sunday school superintendent father.

Dr. Blake is sure he can help me.

Dr. Blake has the answer.

He tells me how to be free of the anguish.

"The one you see within as a fox face is the real you. It is all your suppressed anger. You must let it out. You must become the one within. You must not be afraid to express the rage. It is the real you."

I stare at the floor as I always do.

If I were able to remember, I would be afraid of Dr. Blake. If I were able to remember, I wouldn't be here in his office. An arm around the shoulder as I sat on his soft leather couch one day last week. A comforting hug. An unwanted touch. Another secret to keep. I try hard to forget his unwanted advances, and I succeed. I'm an expert at forgetting.

As I draw invisible circles on the wall of my dorm room at night, the memories of Dr. Blake's inappropriateness obey and recede as they always have. He knows he can help me, but he's wrong. The fox face I see within is not the real me. It couldn't be. I refuse to believe Dr. Blake's words. The presence inside me is murderous. It's dark. It's somehow not even human.

As I sit here now, staring at the floor, I realize something that I didn't know before: Dr. Blake is insane. Everyone is insane.

I also realize that I have two choices. I can try again to end the pain. I've never succeeded before, but maybe I can now. Or I can sit in the front row of the play people call life and watch the insane actors move around the stage.

By God's grace, I choose the latter.

* * * * *

Think. Think.

Concentrate.

Rocking helps, but people will notice.

What's wrong with me?

Am I going crazy?

"Please open your Bibles to Matthew 13."

The visiting chapel speaker lays his massive Bible on the podium and looks out over the gymnasium full of college students.

"The parable of the sower."

The rustle of thin pages begins, then subsides.

Oh, God, please help me hold it together.

Keep me from rocking.

Don't let people notice.

"And as he sowed, some seeds fell beside the road . . ." (Matthew 13:4).

Please. Please. The volcano inside is erupting again. The pressure inside is slowly, immeasurably building. Like the heated air inside a pressure cooker, the silent powerful expanding within begins again. Sometimes it's a certain word or a phrase in someone's sentence; sometimes it's a casual look, someone's distracted glance in my direction; the eyes—it's often the eyes. Sometimes it's a sound or a vaguely familiar smell or a brief scrap of a distant picture in my memory.

Many things trigger the slow upward crest of the wave within. It's like watching the thick oozing of a lava lamp steadily in slow motion moving toward the surface. As the eruption grows, fleeting pictures cascade through my head: tables, a screaming child; burning; silence; wicked faces; evil eyes; hooded ones. Like someone trying to catch up during a slide presentation, the scenes flash with vivid repetition before my mind's eye. The scraps of pictures seem out of place, jumbled. My memory refuses to acknowledge them. They're not mine. They're not of me.

"And the birds came and ate them up" (Matthew 13:4)

My mind runs ahead to what it pictures is about to happen. I see myself stand to my feet and begin beating my head with my flailing fists. I can hear the screams so well hidden inside suddenly erupt and stab the reverent silence. I see the shock on the faces of those turned toward me as the unbearable anguish inside me becomes audible.

"He who has ears, let him hear" (13:9).

Do something!

Do something!

I do what I have done hundreds, no thousands, of times before. The pages of the opened Bible in my lap blur. My eyes run past them and become embedded in the textured grains of the wooden bleachers in front of me. The sounds around me begin to speak to me from a muted distance. My unblinking eyes turn what they see into a black-and-white photographic negative. The light colors around me become black, and the dark colors become light. I can hear my lungs obediently, rhythmically working away as I slip into my self-induced trance.

The soothing comfort, like a fine cool mist, rolls over me. My clenched muscles relax as the numbness mercifully spreads throughout my mind, my body, my soul. Sometimes I need to use my ring to help me get into my trance. The blue rectangular stone in my high-school ring becomes my entrance into the other world, the sealed off one, the one I have often gone to to silence the volcano within.

As I focus on the ring's beveled stone, I slide silently into my trance. Here you can be asleep while awake, unmoving while conscious, unblinking yet aware. But this time I don't need the two-sided door of my ring to transport me to the other side of consciousness. I sit for the remainder of the chapel service in a kind of suspended reality—hearing and seeing, but not touching the world outside. No one notices, and my trance soothes the erupting volcano, at least for the time being.

"In Jesus' name, Amen."

Lord, just help me get back to my room. Coming out of a trance is like a powerful camera lens zooming suddenly into focus. Coming back is easier than getting there. But coming back also awakens the volcano once again.

Lord, please keep me together.

What's happening?

Am I going crazy?

Don't be afraid.

It'll be all right.

* * * * *

"Please, please. Don't let them do this to me."

The pastor's wife is a tiny woman. Her hair is always flipped under in a careful sort of way. Her hands are small and delicate. She has a soft voice.

"Please, please. Don't let them do this to me!"

I've driven the 200 miles to my former pastor's new parsonage. I know that I'm not being helped by Dr. Blake. I know that God has the answer, but the psychologist has not pointed me to God. So I've come here to Pastor Tom's house.

Maybe he can help me.

With a trusting honesty I pour out my anguish to the pastor's wife. I tell her about the anguish within. I tell her about the murderous blackness, the voices, the presence. As we sit together at the kitchen table, the volcano within me begins to erupt. I feel the insanity closing in on me, so I excuse myself and get some fresh air outside.

As I walk along the streets near their house, calm returns. I step through the door. Pastor Tom's wife is starting dinner. We don't talk more about my terror. Dinner is almost ready. Baby Melanie joins the three of us at the table. We talk together about nothing.

Pastor Tom is close to God.

Maybe he can help me.

* * * * *

It's the next morning now. I climb down the carpeted stairs and hug the pastor's wife as I say good morning.

"Pastor Tom wants to see you in his study."

I'm relieved by her words. Maybe he can help me. But as I enter his study I realize that Pastor Tom is not the same soft and kind man I remember. He has a pinched, agitated look on his face as he asks me to sit down across from his desk. Slowly he tilts back in his padded desk chair. The collar on his fitted white shirt is starched at attention. His narrow brown tie is pinned neatly by a cross-shaped tie tack. He fidgets with a paper clip as he stares down at his desk.

"My wife told me about your conversation together last night."

He begins to crush my hope in such a gentle way.

"I am very concerned about what she told me."

I'm glad he's concerned.

I still don't know what he is about to do.

I still believe that maybe he can help me.

As if to emphasize his next point Pastor Tom taps the paper clip loudly on his desk.

"You are a dangerous person. I consider you a threat to my family."

I take in a slow breath to give my mind time to take in what he's just said. The tape recorder in my head is trying to replay his words, but his next words interrupt my growing desperation.

"I've called the mental hospital, and they are coming to get you. I hope they commit you and keep you there for the rest of your life. You're too much of a danger to be around people."

The redness in his face is growing darker.

He stands up as he talks. I can see the anger in his eyes. It reminds me of the look I have seen somewhere before. My father's eyes. I have seen the same look there long ago. The terror inside explodes. The people from the mental hospital are coming. I remember with horror the state mental hospital we visited two years ago with our senior high sociology class. The patients are housed in an old army barracks. A confused, demented crowd swirls around us as we walk through the locked units. Some drool and wave their hands in our faces. Others scream and bite their arms, rocking erratically back and forth.

"I've called the mental hospital . . ."

My mind has a hard time getting past Pastor Tom's sentence. My eyes leave his face and stare for a minute at the floor. The merciful numbness in my mind is beginning to wear off.

Think. Think.

Help me, God! Help me!

As I stand up and walk out of Pastor Tom's study, I meet his wife. In desperation, I take her by her shoulders and shake her as the words come tumbling out of my mouth.

"Please, please, don't let them do this to me! I'm not crazy! Please! I'm not crazy!"

Later, as my mind replays this scene over and over again, I realize that when a person is trying desperately to prove that they're not crazy, they look more and more crazy the harder they try to prove that they are sane. But now, in the intensity of the moment I don't realize this. I'm looking into the eyes of the pastor's wife. She stares blankly back at me. I've seen that look somewhere before, long ago. My mother's eyes.

"We've called the college, and they told us that they have never heard of Dr. Blake."

I stare in unbelief as Pastor Tom speaks.

"Please believe me! There really is a Dr. Blake! Please, please call the president of the school. He knows about Dr. Blake! He will tell you that I'm not lying! Please!"

As I beg, somewhere inside me hopelessness gains ground. It will not matter that later President Kelly confirms my story or that the men from the mental ward don't arrive to take me away. It will not matter that Pastor Tom calls my father and tells him of my mental problems. It will not even matter that my father's reaction when I get home will become another incident of horror I have to forget.

Nothing will matter anymore. I went believing that Pastor Tom might help me. I came away knowing that if I tell a Christian about the anguish within, they will try to have me committed. Silently, almost unknowingly, I vow never to tell my secrets to another Christian.

Somewhere inside me the hopelessness gains more ground.
"Please, please don't let them do this to me."

M y world is falling apart. I can't keep going for too long with things the way they are now. Confusion. Blank places in my day. Fragments of hideous pictures cascading uncontrollably through my mind. Strange feelings. Terror for no reason. Not being able to breathe. Voices inside. Loud voices. Screaming.

And then there is the cold, silent mask of death over everything. It seems to fill every part inside. Like a mysterious fog settling low to the ground, the feeling of death rolls in, covering all my thoughts.

My inner confusion has become more and more obvious to others. The dean of women here at the college has heard reports of my strange behavior. I've been seen running in terror through the woods near the school. I have gone missing for several days at a time. As people question me about these things, I don't have any recollection of them. I was not around when they were happening. I must have been somewhere deep inside, cut off from reality. Their questions about why I did something only add to my confusion and frustration.

God, please help me. I believe only You can unravel this. Only You can fix what's going wrong inside. Show me what is going on. Why am I like this, Lord? Why? I can't go on like this anymore.

The thought of death becomes as anticipated as a long cool drink of lemonade on a hot, steamy August afternoon. Death is my friend. Death will bring relief from this insanity. Death will keep me from going crazy.

"Nothing can separate you from His love; life can't, death can't, the angels won't, and all the powers of hell itself cannot separate you from the love of God which is in Christ Jesus our Lord" (Romans 8:38, author paraphrase).

I've been reading my Bible every morning and trying to pray. I'm memorizing Scripture, and this verse is the one I've chosen to learn next. But as I study it, the "angel of light," as the Bible calls Satan, begins to twist the truth. I can hear thoughts in my head. They're telling me that the verse is true. They're saying that nothing, not even death, can separate me from God. Not even death. So why don't I go ahead and end my life?

It's part of God's plan.

It's His way.

He wants me to die.

It will end the anguish.

It will stop the pain.

It's the only way.

It's God's way.

Choose it.

Choose it now before it's too late.

God wants you to.

Finally, finally, the torment will be over.

Death will be a friend to you.

Finally you will have peace.

* * * * *

Please, God, hang on to me.

I'm going under again, Lord.

The waves of terror and panic are once again washing over me.

Hang on to me, Lord.

That's all I can say, all I know to do as I feel myself going under once again. I'm sinking down somewhere inside, away from the sounds and touch of things around me. It's happened hundreds, maybe thousands, of times before for as long as I can remember. Just lately, it's been happening more and more frequently. I can't explain what happens. I can only hang onto God and watch it happen.

It's a feeling of movement inside. Then comes the same sensation I get as I'm drifting off to sleep at night. I'm losing control. I'm receding somewhere inside. It's as though I'm blacking out, blanking out. I remember feeling the same drifting and the same panic when at five, I have my tonsils removed. I look up from the table as the ether mask is placed over my mouth and nose.

"Can you count to ten for me?"

The tall man in the white coat stands beside the table where I lie getting ready for the operation.

"One . . . two . . . three. . . ." I begin to go under. The numbness is washing over my mind, just as it is doing now as the terror inside grows. It feels the same.

A mental anesthesia.

I'm going under again, Lord.

Please, God, hang on to me.

The picture comes quickly to my mind now as it always does when I'm sinking into somewhere inside. It's from the Creator God, the God of the Bible. I can see His hand, palm facing toward the sky, reaching out for me. It's the hand of the gentle

Shepherd in my Sunday school picture of long ago, a strong hand, a safe hand. Then I see myself, a terrified little girl, nestled down inside His cupped hand. Slowly, tenderly, He clasps His hands together with me hidden inside. It's His way of showing me, reminding me, where I really am. Safe. Protected. In His hands, covered over from the terror and confusion that follows.

After I've been under for a while, I somehow come back to my mind once again. Sometimes I'm in a different room, a different apartment. But this time, I'm outdoors. It's night, but the darkness is lightened by the full moon. The sky is cloudless. I am in a clearing, in a field. Tall slender trees form a hedgerow outlining its edges. Beyond the trees tiny lights shine in faraway houses. Their lights blink as the trees in front move slightly in the gently blowing breeze.

There's a group of people near one edge of the field. Ten, perhaps twenty. My eyes scan their silhouettes as I slowly walk up behind them. They're all facing one way, all focused on one event. At first their heads and shoulders block my view. But as I get closer, I can see through cracks between them. There's a light up in front. The people form a circle around something in the center. There's an invisible presence here in this place. Every part of me is chilled by it. Its weight presses down on the air, on me. It's a very, very familiar pressure, a recognizable heaviness. The alarm inside me goes off, desperately trying to warn me. There is wickedness here.

Run! Run!

But it's too late.

In an instant the entire scene comes into focus. I'm completely aware now. The fog inside has cleared and all of my senses are filling out the drama, the tragedy, as it unfolds before me. The murmuring undertones I had heard before now turn into chanting. The pressure of the presence I felt now grows so intense that it seems to agitate the people before me toward a climactic frenzy.

Run! Run!

My mind pleads with my stone feet to escape, but I can't move. Through the crack of space between those in front of me I see him. There is a long-robed hooded man. There is a baby. I see his outline as he lifts the little one with raised hands toward the sky. The rhythmic chanting grows louder. But above it I can hear the hooded one's voice.

"We offer this one to you, oh shining one. . . ."

At these words, a forgotten memory within me explodes and rushes to the front of my mind. I see another man—my father—with raised hands. I see another little one—a small girl—being lifted high above his head. My father's voice echoes in my mind with the same words I now hear.

"Be pleased, oh mighty one, by this sacrifice."

Like the twisted threads in a rope, my mind entwines the two scenes—the one here before me now and the one from long ago.

It's me! It's me! It's me!

The silent, wrenching screams within seem to block out the hideousness I now witness. I am numb. It's as though my mind mercifully dulls me to the sharpness of my own memory. I turn away from the scene my eyes are looking at here in the field, but I can't turn away from the horror of the awakened memory within.

* * * * *

Time has passed. I'm sitting cross-legged on my bed now in the dorm rocking from side to side. I am trying to stay sane. When I first returned from the woods that surround the school, I frightened my roommates with my wild look, my confused mind, my rambling words. Now I'm silent. The school nurse has been called. Hysteria, they call it. I tell no one of the incident I've just witnessed in the field. I tell no one of the incident I've just remembered from the farm.

Oh, God, hang on to me.

Keep me from going crazy.

The Lord is my shepherd, I shall not want. . . . He restores my soul. . . . Even though I walk through the valley of the shadow of death . . . Thou art with me . . . . The baby! The little one I saw in the woods. He's dead! He's dead! But I'm still alive, God, still alive! It could have ended the same way for me when I, too, was a little one in my father's outstretched arms. But it didn't. God, You were there.

"Greater is He who is in [me], than he who is in the world" (1 John 4:4).

* * * * *

I can see the rain on her face.

More strange things have been happening to me. I've been noticing that I am missing time. When I look at the clock, it's 2 o'clock on Monday. When I look a few minutes later, it's 5 o'clock on Friday. Where has the time gone? What have I been doing? Where have I been?

I can see the rain on her face.

The phrase keeps running through my mind. What does it mean? I've been hearing strange things. I've been doing strange things. Whenever it rains, something inside me explodes. I watch myself race through the rain and out into the woods that surround the school. It's as though a terrified someone is living within me, and she sees the rain as a signal for insanity.

I can see the rain on her face.

Please, God, help me.

Somewhere in the back of my mind, I recognize what's going on. Somewhere inside, these bleeps, these missing spaces in my life, seem familiar. One minute I'm taking a history exam, and the next I look up and I'm in someone's apartment eight hours away from the school. How did I get here? Who are these people that seem to know who I am? Where am I? I've become very skillful at asking questions that will help me learn the answers. Eventually, I'll learn that I've driven here in my car. I'll stop at a gas station, pretending that I need directions, so that I can tell which state I'm in.

Please, God, help.

Sometimes I seem to be dreaming even though I'm awake. I dream of a room in the library. I dream of the narrow, musty smelling shelves. I dream of some of the other students and two of our professors coming with a key at night and unlocking the little room. There is something vaguely familiar about the dark presence in that little room. It will be another thirty years before I hear the president of our college confirm what my mind sees in that little room at the library. He will tell of faculty members who encourage the students to read occult books and act out rituals in a nearby field, and he will tell of the dark events that go on in the room I now see only in my daymares.

I have other daydreams too. Somewhere in the back of my mind I seem to know that I am at the center of some kind of group, some kind of power structure that includes some of the students in my class. I have a strange feeling that I know what it's like to be at the center of whatever this is. I have been here before. I have sensed the same dark presence before.

Please, God, help.

I have a feeling that there is some kind of place inside me, like a power outlet in the wall, into which something that will let my power flow wants to be plugged. What is it?

Please, God, help.

* * * * *

God has the answer.

Somewhere inside of me I'm still holding on. In spite of Pastor Tom, in spite of Dr. Blake, in spite of everyone, I still have within me the hope that God must have the answer to all of this confusion. But I don't know how to find Him. I can't tell other Christians about what's going on inside, or they, like Pastor Tom, will have me committed to a mental hospital. And I can't find God from someone who doesn't believe in Him.

I wait.

I pray.

God has the answer.

Like a gift from God, the hope within has kept me going, kept me trying, kept me alive. And I've been busy, very busy, with a double major and working the five to midnight shift. Now I'm off to graduate school in another state. The loneliness and confusion seem to be even worse than before.

A Christian group has a table at the freshman orientation. I've heard of their campus ministry before. The man behind the table is very outgoing and friendly. He invites me to a beginning-of-year picnic they are sponsoring. I go. I pretend to be normal. I have watched lots of my classmates. I've studied how they act as a way to learn how to keep the insanity I sense within me from showing on the outside. Most of the time I do a good job.

I start going to the regular meetings the campus ministry holds. I like how they seem to know God. I like how they seem to want to help. I wish I could tell them. But I can't. If I do, they will try to have me committed.

There's one woman on the staff who disciples the women students. Brenda has a quick smile and a ready laugh. I'm getting to know her. She's the one I call when it rains, when the insanity within rushes to the surface.

"Don't ask any questions, just pray for me," I tell her.

My request must sound a bit mysterious, but it's the only way I can ask for help. I want someone to be praying for me while my mind is away, wherever it goes, when it begins to rain. I will find myself sometime later, clothes soaked, terrified and exhausted from running from something I can't see, something I can't remember. I know that God has the answer for the insanity inside of me. Maybe this lady can help me find His answer.

But one night the insanity is hard to disguise. It begins to rain as Brenda drives me home from a Bible study. She slows to a stop in front of my dorm, and I step outside the car. The raindrops touch my face.

I can see the rain on her face.

I hear that same sentence inside my head every time it rains and my face gets wet. I begin to feel the confusion take over. I don't go into the dorm. Instead, I wander in a kind of stupor out in the parking lot, oblivious to the falling rain. I stare at Brenda as she asks if I am all right. I don't answer. My eyes must look as strange on the outside as they seem to me on the inside.

I don't say anything as she helps me back into the car. I ride silently as she takes me to Jim's house. Jim is the head of the campus ministry here at our university. He and his wife are very gracious as they welcome this bizarre-behaving, rain-soaked woman standing at their front door. They make arrangements to have me meet with the other staff members tomorrow.

I don't know where I spend the night. I only know that now I'm in a small upstairs apartment that serves as home and office for some of the ministry staff. We're waiting for someone to arrive. I don't know who. We sit and talk small talk together. I notice that there is a familiar voice speaking on the television. With his North Carolina accent, the evangelist reads slowly from the Bible he holds in front of him.

The television camera scans the large stadium as hundreds of people stream down the aisles toward the famous preacher. As the choir sings "Just as I Am," and Billy Graham bows in silent prayer, the volcano inside me begins to erupt. The powerful message of the gospel he speaks of and the verses he reads aloud to the packed stadium incite a rage within me. The murderous presence that has lived within me for as long as I can remember hisses out a statement to the startled staff members sitting around the coffee table.

"She belongs to us! We own her! She is ours!"

I haven't said these words, but I hear them come from my own mouth as if it were under the control of another. The voice is not my voice. It's a low, guttural sound from somewhere deep within me. I'm both frightened by it but also familiar with it. I've heard that voice before. It's come many times from my father.

I don't remember much of what else goes on. But I leave with a promise from the staff members that they will meet with me again soon. What has just happened in this small upstairs apartment is the most dramatic turning point in my life. God's promised healing has begun.

Don't be afraid.

It'll be all right.

God has the answer.

THIRTEEN

his must be a dream. I see Darrel, Dan and several other ministry staff sitting across from me intently reading the Bible aloud to me. They're reading verses about life and Christ's victory over death. Maybe these truths can evict the demonic presence of suicide and death that is so strong within me.

"Why don't you begin reading here at verse one of John 11?"

Darrel leans forward and hands the Bible to me. Like an explosion, the powers within me heave it across the room. It smashes against the opposite wall. The power of the Word of God is so real to the demonic presence within me that even touching it causes this violent reaction.

Darrel himself begins to read: "Now a certain man was sick, Lazarus of Bethany, the village of Mary and her sister Martha" (11:1). I sit as though I'm in a trance as the story of Christ's power over death unfolds through the words of Scripture. It seems like all my senses are on high alert. The ticking of the clock on the wall is so loud in my head that it's hard to concentrate on Darrel's words. The other sounds in the apartment seem to be magnified as well.

If you listen to them, we'll kill you!

The threats of violence against me that I hear inside my head aren't new to me. They've been with me ever since I was little. But now as I sit here with these men, something has changed. I'm not alone. It's not just me versus the voices anymore. These people want to help me. They must have been sent by God.

God, don't let them give up on me.

Please help them.

Show them what to do.

Show them how to help me.

This must be a dream.

I'm not alone anymore.

* * * * *

Death. Death.

There's a life-and-death battle going on inside of me. I've met several times with Dan and Darrel. Each time they use the truths from the Bible against the darkness within me. The more they shine God's light at the darkness, the more the darkness tries to destroy me. It's as though the terrorists within are determined to kill their hostage before they themselves are destroyed.

Death. Death.

The desire to die is so strong now within me that it can only be called a lust. It's with me all the time. When I walk by a window, I have to make sure my feet keep me walking straight ahead. Otherwise, they'll carry me to the window, and I'll find myself standing on the sill ready to jump.

Death. Death.

I'm able to steal medications. I take prescriptions for serious illnesses like heart disease or powerful pain killers. I call the poison control center at the local hospital and tell them that my roommate has just taken an overdose. What should I do? Should I bring her into the emergency room? I listen with a calmness that often comes before someone is about to end his or her life.

"If she's taken more than three," the nurse on the other end of the phone tells me, "bring her in immediately. More than three of these pills will be fatal."

Without saying good-bye, I hang up the phone and take ten of the small yellow pills from the prescription bottle. I have to be sure I take enough. With only God's angels watching over me, I wake up in my apartment three days later, still alive. Desperation changes to frustration as I realize that once again God has not allowed me to die.

Death. Death.

I'm driving down Leeland Street now. There's a trailer truck coming towards me in the opposite lane. The lust that drives me toward death takes over again. My eyes focus on the shiny chrome grill on the front of the truck as I turn my steering wheel counterclockwise. I will meet him in a head-on collision. Then it will all be over. But the angels are again watching over me. I quickly turn the steering wheel until it won't turn to the left anymore, but my car keeps moving straight ahead in my own lane as the truck roars safely by.

Death. Death.

There's an inner force within me that insists that I should die. I am in agreement with it. Death will end the torment once and for all. But God's angels are near too. They are watching as I slowly move the razor blade across my wrist. A gash opens up on each side, to the left and to the right of the vein, but it's as though there's an invisible finger covering my vein. Ten . . . fifteen . . . twenty . . . and still the cuts appear only on either side of the vein, leaving it uncut.

Death. Death.

But God's angels are near.

* * * * *

"They came to the other side of the sea, into the country of the Gerasenes" (Mark 5:1).

It's been six months since I first met the people on the campus ministry team. My life has been a series of confusing and bizarre events with a small amount of sanity mixed in between.

"When He got out of the boat, immediately a man from the tombs with an unclean spirit met Him. . . . Constantly, night and day, he was screaming among the tombs and in the mountains, and gashing himself with stones" (5:2-5).

The nights are the worst. The torment gets so intense that it drives me like the man of the Gerasenes in the Gospels. He was driven by the forces within him into the wilderness. The tormentors inside me drive me out into the darkness of the night.

"Seeing Jesus from a distance . . ." (5:6).

Churches. I'm drawn to churches. Their lighted steeples point upward toward the dark sky. I don't know why I am sitting here in the parking lot staring up at the bright cross at the top of the steeple. Almost in the same way as the lust to die drives me, there is another powerful force that seems like a magnet within. It doesn't drive me—it draws me. It draws me now to this church, to this cross.

Somehow I feel a comfort here. Like I have done on other nights, I'll break into this church and sleep in the balcony. Somehow it makes me feel safe. If I sleep up here, I can go unnoticed in case I'm still asleep when the pastor arrives in the morning. I can quietly leave through a side door while I hear him moving around in his office.

I arrive back at my apartment in the morning, but the anguish is still there. Sometimes the confusion gets so overwhelming that I have trouble remembering who I am. I'm also always afraid that someone may have seen me hiding in the church. What if I meet him somewhere and he recognizes me? Then he'll know I'm crazy.

Later in the day, the volcano within me seems to unexpectedly erupt. I have to run, to get away. I have to escape, but I'm not sure what I'm running from. Maybe Brenda can help calm the volcano inside me. Maybe she will pray with me like she often does. But when I arrive at her apartment, the pressure inside only gets worse. I have to run. I have to get away. I don't notice the stares of Brenda's neighbors as I bolt out of her apartment into the snowy yard. I don't feel the snow or patches of ice beneath my bare feet. I just stare straight ahead as if in a trance as Brenda tries to coax me back into the house.

"Constantly, night and day, he was screaming among the tombs and in the mountains . . ." (5:5).

Hang on to me, Jesus.

* * * * *

I'm alone again, God.

Help me, God. Help me.

It's 11 o'clock at night, and they're here again. I can hear them chanting outside my apartment. The "Process People," as they call themselves, are here at the university. They say they are worshipers of Lucifer. They've come, somehow knowing that I'm here. They're trying to scare me, I think.

Make me strong, God.

Keep me safe.

What should I do, God? All my friends from the campus ministry have left for the summer. They're all at their headquarters working until next fall. I'm alone in a different way now, God. Before, when I was alone, I didn't know what the terror on the inside was all about. But now I know what the real problem is. I know about the enemy. I know he wants to destroy me. I know he has already tried to destroy me on the inside.

God, don't let him win.

I'm sitting at my desk in my tiny studio apartment.

Something bizarre is happening.

The paneling on the walls is closing in on me.

Am I hallucinating?

What's going on?

Are the chanters I hear outside doing this?

I'm alone, God. Help me, God. Help me.

Breathe deeply.

Don't panic.

Don't panic.

I can't go on like this.

There's no one who understands, no one to talk to about this craziness. Every time I look at the walls they seem to move toward me, trying to crush in on me.

Suicide.

It's the only answer.

The little brown prescription bottle I've stolen is sitting here on my desk. The pills inside rattle as I shake it. It would be so easy, so calming, so final. No more terror. No more anguish. No more wrestling with invisible things. The escape plan of death has never worked before. God has never let it work. I've begged Him, yelled at Him, pleaded with Him to let it work, to let me die. But each time He says no. Maybe this time He'll see that death is my only answer.

Sometimes when you're on the edge of sanity, leaning over the pit called death, a strange giddiness comes upon you. I can feel that now as I half mockingly make a plan. Even a prisoner gets one phone call. I'll call a pastor and tell him what the problem is. If he says he can't help me, then I'll kill myself. As I speak these words to myself out loud there's a lightheartedness, a desperate kind of humor that seems to take over. It's as though I'm drunk and making a game of trying to stay alive.

The yellow pages of the phone book have a familiar smell as I turn to the section where all the churches are listed. Each church includes the name of its pastor. I close my eyes and run my finger slowly down the list. I open my eyes. My finger has stopped at "Reverend Joseph Beal." In my confusion, it seems logical to call this man whom I have never heard of and ask him my question.

When he answers the phone, I check to make sure that he really is a pastor. He tells me that he is, so I go on to explain the reason I've called.

"This may sound strange to you, but I have a problem. It's not a mental problem or even an emotional problem. It's a spiritual problem. It's a problem with wicked spirits. They're inside of me. I know God has the answer, but I don't know how to find it. If you say you can't help me, I'm going to end my life."

My words sound so calm, so unattached from me. I sound like an uninvolved reporter instead of a desperate person about to murder herself.

"You know, I think that there's a lot of that kind of thing going on in the churches these days. We really need to be more on top of it, I guess. But I'm sorry, I can't help you."

I can't help you.

I can't help you.

The pastor's words are like an instant tape recording in my head. Maybe he didn't understand me.

"Do you realize that, if you say you can't help me, I'm going to end my life?"

I try to make it very clear.

"Yes, and I feel very badly about that, but I'm afraid I can't help you."

Even when you're straddling the dividing line between life and death, there seems to be at least a small part inside that wants to live. As the pastor ends the call, that part in me has just died. But just as I'm putting down the receiver, I hear his voice again.

"Wait, wait!"

I move the receiver back up to my ear and listen.

"I was at a missions conference last month, and I heard a missionary from Africa speak about the witchcraft there. Maybe he can help you. I'll try to contact him and ask him to call you."

In my confusion, I haven't really understood how dramatic this phone call has been. It's as though the Lord has carefully protected the thin spider web that has been connecting me with life. As I cautiously give the pastor my phone number, I set the little bottle of pills back away from me on my desk. At least for now I'll wait on my plan.

Help me, God. Help me.

aybe there is hope.

"Is Laura there?"

The voice on the other end of the telephone is a man's voice. I don't recognize it, but I don't ask any questions. I don't need to know who it is.

"Laura doesn't live here anymore."

I hear my voice say the words as though I'm somewhere miles away. Before the man has a chance to answer, I quickly hang up the phone. As I turn to finish stirring my dinner on the stove, the phone rings again. It's him. I know it is.

I won't answer it.

I should answer it.

I don't want to answer it.

I can't answer it.

A strange tug-of-war is going on in my mind. It's as though part of me knows something about this call, knows that it's important for me to answer. But there's another part of me, the more-in-control part, that doesn't want to have anything to do with this call or this caller.

Twenty-three . . . twenty-four . . . twenty-five . . . twenty-six rings. The caller is persistent. Thirty-one . . .

thirty-two . . . . Finally the part of me that wants to answer the phone wins. I cautiously pick up the receiver.

"Laura, is that you?"

How does he know? Why did he call back? Later this man will tell me that almost instantly after I hung up the phone, the Lord seemed to tell him that the timid voice he had just heard was Laura's.

"Who are you?"

Something is going on inside me, a fierce battle.

Hang up!

Don't listen to him!

No, I want to talk to him.

"My name is Jim. I'm a pastor. I was given your name by a friend. He told me that you have been having some problems."

For some reason the memories of all the betrayals, all the times people haven't known how to help me, suddenly flood into my emotions.

Don't trust him.

"Are you a Christian?" I ask.

My suspicion, my fear, is getting ready to hang up again.

"Yes, I am."

"Then I can't talk to you. You'll have me committed to a mental hospital."

The vow I made in my pastor's living room not so long ago was still very much in place inside. I don't dare tell a Christian. But the voice on the phone seems to really want to help, to really care about the hell inside of me. But how can I believe him when he says he won't have me committed? Once again the battle inside gets louder and louder. He promises that if I come to see him just once he won't let them lock me away. I agree to go. I scribble the directions to his house sideways on my calendar. Next Tuesday. Two o'clock.

Maybe there is hope.

By the time I open the daybed in my tiny apartment and get ready to go to bed, I've already forgotten his call. I've already forgotten what we talked about. My mind is up to its old tricks. It has had lots of practice at forgetting.

Now it's Tuesday. My calendar puzzles me. It's telling me that I have to be at Jim's house at two o'clock. Who is Jim? Why am I supposed to be at his house at two? When you live your life in unrelated snapshots, it doesn't seem to make sense. This is just another one of those times, those confused places in my life. But the Lord is telling me something inside. He is telling me to go to Jim's house. Follow the directions you wrote out. They will get you there.

It takes me twenty minutes to drive to the little town where I'm supposed to meet Jim. This twenty-minute period is one of the most confused times I've known. My mind is like a battle zone. Thoughts, distractions, anger, fears—all swirl around in my head as I try to drive.

I slow down and drive past the white house on the corner. It's across from the post office, Jim said. I can see the black numbers over the door—116. The numbers match those I've copied from my calendar. But I don't recognize the house. I thought that once I got here maybe I would know, maybe it would make sense why I've driven here. But it all looks unfamiliar, so I drive away.

For a minute I'm confused about how to get back to the city. One block past the white house on the corner there's a little parking place. I park and try to sort things out. What should I do? The gentle pressure inside that I know as God's voice again begins to talk to me.

"Go back to the white house on the corner. That's where you should be. I want you to talk to Jim."

It's only one minute past two as I walk up the sidewalk and knock on the front door. Through the sheer curtains on the window I can see someone coming. I wait as a lady opens the door and smiles at me.

"Hi, Laura. My name is Carol. Jim's out back in his office."

How does she know my name?

How does she know I'm here to see Jim?

Who is Jim?

I follow her back to the small building behind the white house on the corner. It's a tiny room that looks like someone's office. There are two men there. They both get up and introduce themselves. Jim and Carl. I have to remember. It's not nice to forget people's names, but I have trouble with that. I begin to remember Jim's voice. I've heard it somewhere before. I begin to remember something about a promise not to have me committed. We talk together for awhile, but I'm having trouble concentrating. The voices inside my head are trying to make me afraid, trying to make me run out of the office.

"Have you ever been involved with psychic things? Has anyone in your family been involved with witchcraft?"

Jim asks a lot of questions. All my answers are no. I have never been involved with psychic things. No one in my family has ever been involved with witchcraft. No. As far as my mind knows, I'm telling the truth. No, I've had a pretty normal life.

Jim seems uncertain or puzzled about something. Carl has mostly been listening as Jim questions me. Sometimes he glances over at Jim, and their eyes meet. Meanwhile, the voices inside my head are getting louder and louder. I wonder if Jim and Carl can hear them.

An hour has gone by. After we bow our heads and pray, I stand and put on my coat. There seems to be a fog or something numb in my mind. I pick up my purse and walk to the door. As I reach for the doorknob, it's as though a sudden rush of sentences pours out of my mouth.

"Well, of course you know both my grandmothers were witches. And all my aunts have powers. One talks to the dead. One helps people see spirits. I do a lot of those kinds of thing too."

My words are like a glass filled to the brim that suddenly gets bumped. They slosh out over the sides so fast it's as though they haven't had time to go past my mind first. There hasn't been time to stop them. Jim looks surprised as he invites me to sit down again. What we talk about now is hard to remember. But I hear him ask if I would like to come back again and talk some more.

Yes, I would like to come and talk some more.

Maybe there is hope.

*   *   *   *   *

I wonder if they think I'm crazy.

I've been meeting with Jim and Carl every week for several months now. I'm not sure how long we meet. Usually, a few minutes after I go inside the office and sit down, I have one of those bleeps I've always had. One minute I'm bowing my head to pray with Jim, and the next it's several hours later. My hair is wet and matted on my forehead as though I've been sweating. My voice is hoarse, and my eyes feel puffy as though I've been crying.

Sometimes, when I first arrive at his office, Jim asks me about the fresh slash marks on my arms. I can't explain why they're there. I know I've put them there, but I don't know why. At other times Jim turns my arms gently from side to side to see the neat circular rows of teeth marks I've embedded in my own arms. Whenever he asks why, I don't have an answer.

The people in Jim's church pray for me. They fast for me. They hold all-night prayer meetings for me in the white church with the concrete porch. Sometimes they search for me in the streets around the church when I've gone missing again. Sometimes they collect me from the airport when I fly back from someplace I can't remember going to.

I wonder if they think I'm crazy.

Spiritual warfare. Doing battle. Fighting for my life. Fighting for my sanity. Many words describe how these brothers and sisters in the Lord join me as I struggle against the darkness within. Jim says we're making some progress. It's hard for me to tell. I only know that the volcano inside seems ready to erupt. I only know that my mind feels like it's on the edge of insanity. I only know that God is hanging on to me.

But I'm leaving.

Before I came to the white house on the corner, I'd already signed a teaching contract at a school in another state. I don't want to go and teach there. I can't. I'm too confused. I decide I have to go, but only for a short time. That way I can break my contract with the Christian high school that is expecting me to come. I seem a bit in a fog as I say goodbye to Jim, to Carl, to the church folk.

I'll be back soon.

Don't worry.

It'll be all right, I assure myself.

Before my first day of classes in my new teaching position, I tell the principal that I have to leave in eight weeks. Something personal has come up. I can't explain the details. But before three days have passed, my mind is doing what it does best. It forgets about my conversation with the principal. It forgets that I'm leaving. It forgets about Jim, about the church, about the warfare. Eight weeks have passed. I'm confused again.

The principal has just informed me that I can pick up my last paycheck in the school office. My last paycheck? Am I being fired? No, he doesn't act as though he's mad. Did I tell him why I was leaving? Yes, we seem to have talked about it sometime before. Like I've had to do so many times before, I play a subtle guessing game with him trying to find out the information that I'm missing. Where am I going? He seems to say that I'm going to another state. But which state? I try to act as though I know all about it.

I wonder if he thinks I'm crazy.

It's moving day now. Some of the teachers from the school have helped me pack. As I start my car, they're standing on the front porch of my apartment building waving at me. I wave back. I have no idea where I'm going. Many times before I've had to figure out how to get back to where I live. I have a whole glove box full of maps from different parts of the country, from different states. I need to check those maps now. Maybe they'll give me a clue as to where I'm supposed to be going. But I have to wait until I drive around the block before I pull them out. Otherwise, my friends waving from the porch might realize that I don't have any idea where I'm moving to.

I drive away. Just after I go around the corner I stop and unfold several of the maps. They don't help.

God, where am I supposed to go?

Help me. Show me. Please, God.

It takes me several days to drive back to the white house on the corner. Each time I come to a big green sign over the highway I ask the only One who is still with me which way I should go. St. Louis or Philadelphia? Indianapolis or Knoxville? Each time the gentle pressure inside makes the choice for me. I drive several hundred miles before I turn onto the little side street and pull up in front of the white church with the concrete porch.

Stop here.

Nothing around me looks familiar. My minds tells me that I haven't seen this church before. But somewhere inside me I know that I'm supposed to be here. I walk up to the small window in the door of the church and look in. A meeting is going on inside. I don't recognize any of the people sitting on the wooden pews. I must have misunderstood God. I must have been wrong. This must not be where I'm supposed to be. So I get back in my car and drive away. But the gentle pressure inside is telling me something again. As I drive away and go around the block, the One inside is telling me to go back to that church with the concrete porch. That's where He wants me to be.

As I quietly enter the back of the church, several people look back and see me. They smile and mouth a silent "Hello." I don't know any of these people.

Why did You bring me here, God?

After the service many greet me with friendly hugs. Two of them tell me that Jim wants to meet with me tomorrow. Who is Jim, and why does he want to meet with me tomorrow? How do these people know me?

I wonder if they think I'm crazy.

I do.

* * * * *

I am hanging on to God.

It's been six weeks since I came back from my teaching job. Jim and Carl have been meeting with me. Sometimes when things get really bad, we meet together several times a week. In many ways things are getting worse.

It's Sunday now. I've just come back from church.

"Where is the Lord God of Elijah?" Jim has just preached a sermon on the challenge between the prophets of Baal and the prophet Elijah. God is powerful. God is greater than all. No one can overpower Him.

As I sit here on the sofa, I'm suddenly aware of a presence in the room. I've felt that presence many times before. I hear myself speaking out loud. But it isn't me. It's that other voice, the one who speaks through me, even if I don't want him to.

"Where is the Lord God of Elijah? Why don't you call on Him? Why don't you ask Him to stop us from cutting you? Let's see if He is as strong as we are."

The mocking challenge within me is clear.

Please, God. Help me.

Don't let them do this to me.

I know that You are stronger.

You are greater.

You are the Lord God of Elijah.

"Help me, Lord. Stop them."

Even as I'm praying, I watch myself walk to the bathroom, open the medicine cabinet and reach for the razor blades.

Please, God. Help me.

The pain doesn't reach me. I quote the verses I've learned. I pray. I expect God to stop them. But He doesn't. But He does do a miracle. He does what He has done many times since I was a child. He makes a special place, a box inside me. It's the box where I put all the things I don't understand, all the things that don't make sense.

The mocking voices erupt in me again.

Where is He?

Why didn't He stop us?

I thought He was the most powerful one of all!

I answer with the answer that I have spoken to others and to myself many times before. By His grace, I make my choice.

I don't know why He didn't stop you, but I still choose Him!

Laura

I am hanging on to God.
God is hanging on to me.

FIFTEEN

"The wicked plots against the righteous and gnashes at him with his teeth. The Lord laughs at him, for He sees his day is coming" (Psalm 37:12-13).

"I would have despaired unless I had believed that I would see the goodness of the LORD in the land of the living. Wait for the LORD; Be strong, and let your heart take courage; Yes, wait for the LORD" (27:13-14).

I say these verses over and over again. I know that the Lord has given them to me for this time, for this battle. It has been getting more and more intense. But there is a sensing within me that God is going to do something. God is going to do something soon. I don't know why I believe that. I only know that it's as though these two verses are a clue, an encouragement, for me. Everything else seems to be getting worse.

"But God . . ."

Jim says that he senses it too.

God is up to something.

We're on the verge of something.

Something important.

I'm meeting with him today.

The battle is as intense as ever.

But something happens.

"There is something important, Jim, something in the deep," I tell him part way through our time together.

The "deep" is the word I use for the hidden place way inside. It's the same place my mind goes when I'm asleep at night. It holds things my mind has never known, never been able to remember. Some of the things we've discovered in the deep have been placed there years ago by my father when he hypnotized me. They're different than memories. My mind doesn't know about them, but they are things that somehow control me.

Jim's prayer is so simple, so uncomplicated, so powerful.

"Lord, we ask You to reveal the hidden things. Show us what is in the deep. By faith, we open the trapdoor that covers it. We expose all to the light of the Son of God."

Inside it's as though a bright light has been turned on. Things scurry away to hide from the light. The volcano inside begins to erupt. The "little men," as I've come to call the spirits within me, are afraid. I can feel their terror. I can sense their rage.

The covenant! The covenant!

I know what that sentence in my mind means. I've always known about the covenant. My grandmother's covenant. But for some reason I've never spoken of it to anyone. I've known about it all along, but it's as though there's been a blanket covering it, keeping it hidden. The story behind the covenant has always been known in my family. My mother's mother was dying. She was in the hospital. There was no hope. Cancer. Twenty-seven years old. Incurable.

A miracle. A healing. Another chance to live. My grandmother has spoken of it often to us all. She knows who has healed her. She speaks about the commitment she has made.

"I have given the first daughter of Maria Louise. She will take my place. I will be healed. She will be given to the one that spoke to me in my hospital room."

The price my grandmother paid for her healing is one that I, the first daughter of Maria Louise, have had to pay. Through her encounter in her hospital room with the dark prince, as she called him, my grandmother has given me an assignment that I am powerless to oppose. I am to belong to them. I am to take her place. My life is exchanged for hers.

"In the name of Jesus Christ, we cancel and destroy any covenant, any pact that was made for Laura by her grandmother. . . ."

Something, someone, is leaving me. I can feel it somewhere deep inside. There is movement. There is an emptying. There is release. For the first time in my life, I can see clearly with my eyes. I can see colors, I can see faces, I can see with a sharpness, a clearness I've never had before. It's as though I've spent my entire life standing with my face pressed up against a screen door. The shadows of the screen pattern have always been between me and the rest of the world.

But now I can see.

I'm fully here.

I'm free!

Today is January 14th. My "D" day, I call it. My deliverance day. The day that I'm finally free to actually experience the change that came when I was just seven years old. Back then I chose Christ. I was transferred out of the kingdom of darkness and into the kingdom of God's Son. Now today, for the first time, I have felt that freedom, that ownership by the Son, that joy.

"I would have despaired unless I had believed that I would see the goodness of the LORD in the land of the living. Wait for the LORD; Be strong, and let your heart take courage; Yes, wait for the LORD" (Psalm 27:13-14).

* * * * *

God is so good.

I feel like I'm dreaming . . . floating . . . quietly watching myself living. It's as though I've come up for air for the first time in my life. Since my "D" day, things have gotten better and better. That terrible pressure, the feeling that there wasn't enough room inside of me, has not returned. Instead, there's a new peace inside, a new confident quietness.

"Had it not been the LORD who was on our side . . . they would have swallowed us alive. . . . Our soul has escaped as a bird out of the snare of the trapper; the snare is broken and we have escaped" (Psalm 124:2, 3, 7).

God is so good.

For the first time, I feel like I'm a human being. I feel like I'm alive. I feel like I have been taken out of a dark tunnel into the light. Sometimes I sense the "little men," the evil spirits inside of me. I can hear them talking. There aren't very many of them left, but they hate it when I think or talk about God, especially when I worship and exalt "the Lion of the tribe of Judah." But Jim has been teaching me how to get rid of them. When I sense that they are there, I grab them in my mind and command them to leave in the name of Jesus Christ. They have to go where He sends them.

Sometimes it seems like they're screaming inside of my head. Sometimes they mock me and take a defiant stand. Sometimes I ask God to show me what they are still holding onto. They resist, but eventually they all leave. Mopping up, I call it—cleaning out the house.

God is so good.

He's teaching me. He's teaching me what it means to be alive. He's teaching me what is a normal part of life and what is bizarre. He's beginning to rebuild me, to heal my emotions.

God is so good.

* * * * *

He isn't supposed to die yet. He's only thirty-one. His wife isn't even thirty. What about his little girl and her younger brother? God, please. He isn't supposed to die yet.

"How's she doing?"

I can hear Bob talking to Sarah on the porch. He's talking about me. It's the day of Jim's funeral. Bob wants to know how I'm doing. It's been only eight months since Jim helped me get free from the darkness. And now he's dead. Unexpected. Tragic. Confusing. So many different words people use to explain the unexplainable.

He isn't supposed to die yet. The illness . . . the hospital . . . the improvement . . . the unexpected turn for the worst . . . the phone call . . . the rush to the hospital . . . the waiting . . . the "I'm so sorry" from the doctor.

Before Jim died, he talked with his young wife about several things. One of them was about me. He said that he wanted me to move in and be part of his family after his death, partly to help out with the two children, partly to be there with his wife, but also to have a place for me to belong.

"How's she doing?" Bob wants to know.

Grieving . . . feeling empty inside . . . feeling like I've lost a good friend . . . knowing somehow that God will keep doing what He has set His heart on doing—"making up for the years that the locusts have eaten."

I'm learning how to be normal.

So many things here at my new family are different than I've ever known: Sarah, Carol and the children all eating together around a table; hearing footsteps in the hall without having someone come to hurt me; no rages; nothing being thrown around the room; being safe at night; no longer surrounded by the darkness.

I'm learning how to be normal.

But some of the voices are still with me. They're not from the vicious, spewing, demonic presence. They're something different. Or are they? Some of them have been with me as far back as I can remember. They're the same voices and feelings I've always had when I had my bleeps on the farm. These voices don't seem to mind when I worship the Lord. They don't have that black, evil feeling around them. Somehow they're different. I can carry on a conversation with them if I want to. But I don't usually. I'm suspicious.

What are they?

Are these voices part of me?

Are they wicked spirits in a clever disguise?

Yes, that's it. They must be wicked spirits who somehow have a nice side to them. I try to get rid of them as Jim had taught me—in the name of Jesus Christ—but they don't leave. Sometimes I can hear them praying to someone they call "the God of the Bible, not the god in the sky."

God, I'm confused.

One of the elders in our church knows about the voices and the times when confusion seems to take over.

"I've heard about something called multiple personality disorder," he told me one day. "A pastor in Kansas who works with people coming out of the occult has come across something that doesn't seem to be a demon. Maybe that's the same kind of thing that you're experiencing."

I'm suspicious. Carl admits that he doesn't know anything more about this "disorder." But we both agree to pray about the possibility. I'm convinced that we're being deceived even by praying about MPD, as it's called. I believe that these voices are a clever trick of the enemy. They're really demons in disguise. Thinking about things like MPD is flirting with psychology. And I know that psychology can be man's attempt to deal with things when he refuses to let God deal with him.

God, keep us from being deceived.

Help us know how to get rid of the voices.

Show me from Your Word.

Help me to learn how to be normal.

"Teach me Your way, O LORD; I will walk in Your truth . . ." (Psalm 86:11).

The verse that the Lord points out to me is from the Psalms: "Unite my heart to fear Your name. . . . You have delivered my soul from the depths of Sheol" (86:11, 13). I've been praying all week about whether to believe in MPD or not. As I meet with Carl, it amazes me that the verses the Lord has seemed to single out for me are the same verses that He has given Carl. As the verses say, I've had lies that need to be replaced with truth. I do sense a dividedness, a brokenness inside. There is no question that my soul, my emotions, have been living in a demonically inspired hell for most of my life.

But God, how do I know if I'm being deceived?

"Trust Me. I'll show you."

In one way, I'm glad that the Lord has shown me about the voices. In another way, I wish He hadn't. If I do have what they call MPD, what do I do about it? Carl doesn't know.

God, show us.

Unite my heart to fear Your name.

* * * * *

Hang on to me, God. Hang on to me.

It's happening again. I don't know why the man standing in the produce department is tapping, tapping with the little short stick in his hand.

Tap . . . tap . . . tap. . . .

He must be trying to decide what to buy. But the tapping of the stick against his other hand makes the volcano inside me begin to erupt.

Hang on to me, God. Hang on to me.

Terror . . . confusion . . . a sense of me receding somewhere inside and someone else getting stronger. It's happening again, only these days I don't sense the presence of the darkness as I did before. I only sense an incredible anguish inside.

"Help me, Lord. Help me."

A memory is coming to my mind, another stick—a broomstick; another man—my father. Tapping . . . tapping. . . . My hand instinctively goes up to feel the ridge that stretches above my right eye. I can trace the line of my "stick dent" as I have always called it. I don't know how it came to be there. I don't know why I've always called it my "stick dent"—until today. As I stand here in the grocery store, the volcano of rage inside gets bigger and bigger. I want to lash out and knock all the vegetables off their neat rows. I want to run. I want to scream.

Help me, Lord. Help me.

It's as though I'm in two places at the same time. I'm in the produce department, but I'm in the living room at the farm. I'm watching the shopper tap his stick in his hand and watching my father tap his stick as he walks toward me. I see bright spots inside my head. I see blackness. I feel piercing pains in the right side of my head above my eye.

The movie projector in my mind finishes the memory of the incident on the farm. I come all the way back again to the present, to the grocery store. There's a new sense of rest, of wholeness. Instantly, the link between my mind and my emotions is reconnected as my mind acknowledges the memory. At least one part, one inside fragment, has been reunited with the rest of my mind. One part has merged. One part has taken its rightful place in God's design for my mind.

God, heal my mind.

Heal my emotions.

Put me back together inside.

And He does.

* * * * *

For the next fifteen years it will basically be just the Lord and me working through the memories that flash unexpectedly in my mind. Just like in the grocery store, first there is the flashback, then the acknowledging of the memory, then the healing. But it's very hard to live with the feeling that I'm trying to keep a helium-filled balloon underwater. There's still a volcano of rage just under the surface, and it takes a lot of energy to keep it from erupting.

Several times I embarrass myself in public. Once in the grocery store, I walk past a woman, turn to her and say, "My father has a crack in his head." Another time, I have a bleep as I'm teaching. I come back to reality just in time to see all my students staring at me. What did I say? What happened just now? I don't remember. The voices inside my head and the emotional ups and downs make it difficult for me to keep things under control at my job. In spite of all the healing the Lord has done inside me, by the end of the day I have trouble remembering who I am or where I am.

I learn to cope with the confusion. I tell myself that my mind is having problems just now. It's not important for me to know who or where I am. God knows, and He will keep me safe. I move to a new state. The Lord seems to be nudging me to go to a Christian psychologist. A Christian referral service has suggested that I contact the office of "Dr. Beavers." Dr. Beavers is very different from the other psychologist I went to so many years ago at the college. He begins each session with prayer and asks God to lead us, to keep us from deception, to do His work of healing.

We talk about how when children have been repeatedly, systematically tortured and abused they somehow dissociate within their minds. It's not a choice as much as it's a natural response to indescribable pain. He views that ability as a gift from God to prevent insanity in children. He explains how some people—holocaust victims, prisoners of war and other veterans, people who have lived through horrible, unspeakable atrocities—divide off parts of their emotions and the memories of certain events from the rest of their thinking. Their mind simply tells them that nothing bad has happened.

The voices I hear within, he explains, are part of me. They are the separated places in my mind that hold the memories, the emotions of the abuse. It's as though a mirror was shattered into fragmented splinters. Like the mirror, the fragments within are all part of one whole, one me. Dr. Beavers' explanation makes sense to me. It begins to clear up much of the confusion I've had since I was a little girl. Now I understand what the bleeps have been. Now I understand the miss-

ing spaces of time. Now I understand what the voices are.
Now the flashbacks make sense.

Thank You, God.

Thank You for hanging on to me all these years.

SIXTEEN

I can see the rain on her face.

The sentence that has repeated itself hundreds of times runs through my head as I sit here in Dr. Beavers' office.

God, show us what this is.

What does it mean?

After prayer, my mind begins to see pictures, isolated snapshots. An iron fence lining the narrow, winding road . . . a jogger . . . brown colored leaves. . . .

Lord, we accept only those memories that come from You. We refuse any thoughts that come from Satan.

The snapshots are turning into a movie. As the pieces take their places, my mind pleads with me to believe the sentence it's told me so many times before.

I can see the rain on her face.

Don't believe the movie.

I can see the rain on her face.

Dr. Beavers is sitting quietly as I watch the action in my mind. I see a college student jogging along the black wrought-iron fence. I see her ponytail bobbing up and down as she pumps her arms back and forth.

She has blonde hair . . . just like me.

I see another scene. The girl is walking up behind someone now. The fallen brown leaves lie like a carpet under the trees as she approaches the kneeling man. His back is toward her. As she gets closer, she sees that he is kneeling over something . . . someone. There is a girl lying quietly in the fallen leaves. Her hair is wet with perspiration. Her face is red.

She has been running . . . just like I've been running.

The man is whispering something to her as he reaches out his hand and caresses her face. It's raining.

I can see the rain on her face.

The movie in the woods is abruptly interrupted by another snapshot. It's of a newspaper. I see someone's hands holding it up as they read the headline: Two Slain Near College Campus. Just as quickly, the picture in my mind returns to the woods. Only this time, there's a difference, a knowing, a truth.

It's me!

No, no, my mind seems to scream. It's not me. I can see the rain on her face. If I were the girl lying in the leaves, I wouldn't be able to see the rain on her face. I could have only seen the rain on her face if I was looking at her, not being her.

No, no. It's not me.

God, help me know the truth. Please.

And then I know.

My mind has done as it always has done since I was a little girl. It has split into two people— one watching the terror as though it were happening to someone else and one experiencing the terror firsthand. Both of them are me. Even as my mind protests, I remember the truth. I remember the terror. I remember the running. I remember the falling. I remember it all. I remember seeing the headlines in the local paper a few days later. I remember asking God why I escaped the attack and the other two women didn't.

I remember, and my mind finally rests.

It doesn't have to pretend any longer.

It doesn't have to protect me from the truth.

Instantly, as I sit here in Dr. Beavers' office, I sense something new inside of me. It's as though two out-of-focus images suddenly become one. Another merging, another integration, another coming together.

"Behold, You desire truth in the innermost being, And in the hidden part You will make me know wisdom . . . " (Psalm 51:6).

". . . and you will know the truth, and the truth will make you free" (John 8:32).

* * * * *

God, where were You?

I've asked that same question many times over the past twenty-five years. Where were You when that innocent little girl with her childlike faith really believed that You would stop the footsteps, stop the men, stop the terror? There's a story in the Bible about two sisters who don't understand why God didn't prevent their brother's death. One came with bitterness; the other came worshiping. Like another gift, God gave me the ability to choose the latter. Somehow I've never turned against Him in bitterness, never blamed Him for all the wickedness.

Maybe it's because in my simple black-and-white world I've known that the darkness is from the black side. The awfulness didn't come from the light. I know Him too well to believe that He joyfully watched as that little girl suffered so much. But I know that He could have stopped it, could have prevented it. And so I've come today like I have so many times before to find out His answer.

God, where were You?

Something has prompted me to ask again this morning as I'm getting ready to go to work. I pull the comb through my hair and wonder again if He will answer the unanswerable. I brush my teeth, slip my papers into my briefcase and head for the school. On the way, God answers me. I begin to sense inside that He is giving me the understanding that I have asked for all these years. I pull my car over to the side of the road and listen. His message is clear. Not a voice, but a knowing inside in my spirit. He tells me four things.

"Every time you prayed I heard."

How kind of Him to tell me that! I can still remember as a little girl wondering if I had prayed the right way. The Sunday school teacher hadn't said if we were supposed to pray out loud or not. Maybe God didn't answer, I had reasoned, because I didn't pray out loud.

The second thing God tells me is making big lines of wet tears run down my cheeks.

"Every time you wept, I wept."

So I never was alone after all when I thought no one else could see my tears.

He continues.

"There's no way that you with your finite mind can understand fully why I gave human beings the power to choose either good or evil."

The fourth thing God tells me leads me to a choice.

"Do you trust Me?"

Here beside the road with my car engine still running, I've heard from the God who has kept me alive all these years. His boundaries around my enemy haven't been the boundaries I would have chosen. I would have shortened the chain around the neck of the roaring lion that has sought to devour me. But now I know Him well enough to know that with great thought, with great care, with great love He chained that roaring lion and measured the length of his chain.

Thank You, God, for hanging on to me.

Thank You, God, for keeping me sane.

Thank You, God, for healing me.

Thank You, God, for making up for the years that the locusts have eaten.

> "I will make up to you for the years
> that the . . . locust has eaten" (Joel 2:25).

Appendix A:

A Biblical Basis for Acknowledging the Reality of Satanic Ritual Abuse

Satan—A Real but Defeated Foe

Job 2:1, 3: Again there was a day when the sons of God came to present themselves before the LORD, and Satan also came among them to present himself before the LORD. . . . The LORD said to Satan, "Have you considered My servant Job? For there is no one like him on the earth, a blameless and upright man fearing God and turning away from evil. And he still holds fast his integrity, although you incited Me against him, to ruin him without cause."

Acts 10:38: "You know of Jesus of Nazareth, how God anointed Him with the Holy Spirit and with power, and how He went about doing good and healing all who were oppressed by the devil, for God was with Him."

Romans 16:20: The God of peace will soon crush Satan under your feet.

Hebrews 2:14: Therefore, since then the children share in flesh and blood, He Himself likewise also partook of the same, that through death He might render powerless him who had the power of death, that is, the devil.

Revelation 12:9: And the great dragon was thrown down, the serpent of old who is called the devil and Satan, who deceives the whole world; he was thrown down to the earth, and his angels were thrown down with him.

Revelation 20:2: And he laid hold of the dragon, the serpent of old, who is the devil and Satan, and bound him for a thousand years.

Do Evil Spirits Really Exist?

Matthew 12:43-45: Now when the unclean spirit goes out of a man, it passes through waterless places, seeking rest, and does not find it. Then it says, "I will return to my house from which I came"; and when it comes, it finds it unoccupied, swept, and put in order. Then it goes and takes along with it seven other spirits more wicked than itself, and they go in and live there; and the last state of that man becomes worse than the first. That is the way it will also be with this evil generation.

Mark 1:21-28: They went into Capernaum; and immediately on the Sabbath He entered the synagogue and began to teach. They were amazed at His teaching; for He was teaching them as one having authority, and not as the scribes. Just then there was in their synagogue a man with an unclean spirit; and he cried out, saying, "What business do we have with each other, Jesus of Nazareth? Have You come to destroy us? I know who You are—the Holy One of God!" And Jesus rebuked him, saying, "Be quiet and come out of him!" Throwing him into convulsions, the unclean spirit cried out with a loud voice and came out of him. They were all amazed, so that they debated among themselves, saying, "What is this? A new teaching with authority! He commands even the unclean spirits, and they obey Him." Immediately the news about Him spread everywhere into all the surrounding district of Galilee.

Mark 1:32-34: When evening came, after the sun had set, they began bringing to Him all who were ill and those who were demon-possessed. And the whole city had gathered at the door. And He healed many who were ill with various diseases, and cast out many demons; and He was not permitting the demons to speak, because they knew who He was.

Mark 1:39: And He went into their synagogues throughout all Galilee, preaching and casting out the demons.

Mark 3:10-12: [F]or He had healed many, with the result that all those who had afflictions pressed around Him in order to touch Him. Whenever the unclean spirits saw Him, they would fall down before Him and shout, "You are the Son of God!" And He earnestly warned them not to tell who He was.

Mark 3:14-15: And He appointed twelve, that they would be with Him and that He could send them out to preach, and to have authority to cast out the demons.

Mark 3:22-27: The scribes who came down from Jerusalem were saying, "He is possessed by Beelzebul," and "He casts out the demons by the ruler of the demons." And He called them to Himself and began speaking to them in parables, "How can Satan cast out Satan? If a kingdom is divided against itself, that kingdom cannot stand. If a house is divided against itself, that house will not be able to stand. If Satan has risen up against himself and is divided, he cannot stand, but he is finished! But no one can enter the strong man's house and plunder his property unless he first binds the strong man, and then he will plunder his house."

Mark 6:7: And He summoned the twelve and began to send them out in pairs, and He gave them authority over the unclean spirits.

Mark 6:12-13: They went out and preached that men should repent. And they were casting out many demons and were anointing with oil many sick people and healing them.

Luke 8:1-3: The twelve were with Him, and also some women who had been healed of evil spirits and sicknesses: Mary who was called Magdalene, from whom seven demons had gone out, and Joanna the wife of Chuza, Herod's steward, and Susanna, and many others. . . .

Revelation 12:9: And the great dragon was thrown down, the serpent of old who is called the devil and Satan, who deceives the whole world; he was thrown down to the earth, *and his angels were thrown down with him.*

See also: Mark 5:1-19; 7:24-30; 9:16-30; 9:38-41; Luke 10:17-20; 13:10-17.

Can Satan Oppress Christians?

Genesis 3:1: Now the serpent was more crafty than any beast of the field which the LORD God had made. And he said to the woman, "Indeed, has God said, 'You shall not eat from any tree of the garden'?"

1 Chronicles 21:1: Then Satan stood up against Israel and moved David to number Israel.

Mark 1:13: And He was in the wilderness forty days being tempted by Satan; and He was with the wild beasts, and the angels were ministering to Him.

Mark 8:33: But turning around and seeing His disciples, He rebuked Peter and said, "Get behind Me, Satan; for you are not setting your mind on God's interests, but man's."

Luke 13:16: "And this woman, a daughter of Abraham as she is, whom Satan has bound for eighteen long years, should she not have been released from this bond on the Sabbath day?"

Luke 22:3: And Satan entered into Judas who was called Iscariot, belonging to the number of the twelve.

Acts 5:3: But Peter said, "Ananias, why has Satan filled your heart to lie to the Holy Spirit and to keep back some of the price of the land?"

2 Corinthians 2:10-11: But whom you forgive anything, I forgive also; for indeed what I have forgiven, if I have forgiven anything, I did it for your sakes in the presence of Christ, in order that no advantage be taken of us by Satan; for we are not ignorant of his schemes.

2 Corinthians 11:3-4: But I am afraid that, as the serpent deceived Eve by his craftiness, your minds will be led astray from the simplicity and purity of devotion to Christ. For if one comes and preaches another Jesus whom we have not preached, or you receive a different spirit which you have not received, or a different gospel which you have not accepted, you bear this beautifully.

2 Corinthians 11:14: No wonder, for even Satan disguises himself as an angel of light.

2 Corinthians 12:7: Because of the surpassing greatness of the revelations, for this reason, to keep me from exalting myself, there was given me a thorn in the flesh, a messenger of Satan to torment me—to keep me from exalting myself!

Ephesians 4:26-27: BE ANGRY, AND YET DO NOT SIN; do not let the sun go down on your anger, and do not give the devil an opportunity.

1 **Thessalonians 2:18:** For we wanted to come to you—I, Paul, more than once—and yet Satan hindered us.

1 **Timothy 1:18-20:** This command I entrust to you, Timothy, my son, in accordance with the prophecies previously made concerning you, that by them you fight the good fight, keeping faith and a good conscience, which some have rejected and suffered shipwreck in regard to their faith. Among these are Hymenaeus and Alexander, whom I have handed over to Satan, so that they will be taught not to blaspheme.

1 **Timothy 5:13-15:** At the same time they also learn to be idle, as they go around from house to house; and not merely idle, but also gossips and busybodies, talking about things not proper to mention. Therefore, I want younger widows to get married, bear children, keep house, and give the enemy no occasion for reproach; for some have already turned aside to follow Satan.

2 **Timothy 2:24-26:** The Lord's bond-servant must not be quarrelsome, but be kind to all, able to teach, patient when wronged, with gentleness correcting those who are in opposition, if perhaps God may grant them repentance leading to the knowledge of the truth, and they may come to their senses and escape from the snare of the devil, having been held captive by him to do his will.

James 4:7: Submit therefore to God. Resist the devil and he will flee from you.

1 **Peter 5:8-9:** Be of sober spirit, be on the alert. Your adversary, the devil, prowls about like a roaring lion, seeking someone to devour. But resist him, firm in your faith, knowing that the same experiences of suffering are being accomplished by your brethren who are in the world.

What Does the Bible Say about Occult Activity, Satanic Worship and Ritual Abuse?

Deuteronomy 18:9-14: "When you enter the land which the LORD your God gives you, you shall not learn to imitate the detestable things of those nations. There shall not be found among you anyone who makes his son or his daughter pass through the fire, one who uses divination, one who practices witchcraft, or one who interprets omens, or a sorcerer, or one who casts a spell, or a medium, or a spiritist, or one who calls up the dead. For whoever does these things is detestable to the LORD; and because of these detestable things the LORD your God will drive them out before you. You shall be blameless before the LORD your God. For those nations, which you shall dispossess, listen to those who practice witchcraft and to diviners, but as for you, the LORD your God has not allowed you to do so."

1 Kings 15:13: And he also removed Maacah his mother from being queen mother, because she had made a horrid image as an Asherah; and Asa cut down her horrid image and burned it at the brook Kidron.

2 Kings 3:26-27: When the king of Moab saw that the battle was too fierce for him, he took with him 700 men who drew swords, to break through to the king of Edom; but they could not. Then he took his oldest son who was to reign in his place, and offered him as a burnt offering on the wall. And there came great wrath against Israel, and they departed from him and returned to their own land.

2 Kings 23:5: He did away with the idolatrous priests whom the kings of Judah had appointed to burn incense in the high places in the cities of Judah and in the surrounding area of Jerusalem, also those who burned incense to Baal, to the sun and to the moon and to the constellations and to all the host of heaven.

Jeremiah 19:4-5: "Because they have forsaken Me and have made this an alien place and have burned sacrifices in it to other gods that neither they nor their forefathers nor the kings of Judah had ever known, and because they have filled this place with the blood of the innocent and have built the high places of Baal to burn their sons in the fire as burnt offerings to Baal, a thing which I never commanded or spoke of, nor did it ever enter My mind."

Ezekiel 23:37, 39: "For they have committed adultery, and blood is on their hands. Thus they have committed adultery with their idols and even caused their sons, whom they bore to Me, to pass through the fire to them as food. . . . For when they had slaughtered their children for their idols, they entered My sanctuary on the same day to profane it; and lo, thus they did within My house."

Acts 19:17-19: This became known to all, both Jews and Greeks, who lived in Ephesus; and fear fell upon them all and the name of the Lord Jesus was being magnified. Many also of those who had believed kept coming, confessing and disclosing their practices. And many of those who practiced magic brought their books together and began burning them in the sight of everyone; and they counted up the price of them and found it fifty thousand pieces of silver.

1 Corinthians 10:20: . . . [B]ut I say that the things which the Gentiles sacrifice, they sacrifice to demons and not to God; and I do not want you to become sharers in demons.

Appendix B:

Frequently Asked Questions about Helping Those with Multiple Personality Disorder

Let me begin this section with a disclaimer. I hesitate to give my personal perspective in answer to the following questions because I am obviously giving only an opinion. These answers are not necessarily the correct or only answers to the questions posed here. I also hesitate because it is too easy to fall into the idolatry of looking to someone or something other than God for guidance. He can and will provide answers to such prayers as "Is this true?" or "Does this apply in my situation?"

The only reason I have agreed to include this section is because 1) there are people who need help, 2) Christ is the answer, 3) only true believers in Him have the answer, and 4) His servants sometimes find themselves in a place of trying to help someone with MPD.*

Please note: We have grouped these questions into two categories. The first group of questions deals with *understanding* the problems of MPD. The second group addresses the *implications*. Even though both men and women can have MPD, the greater percentage are women. With this in mind, we will use the pronouns "her" and "she" throughout this section. Since other personalities within the person may speak, those terms also apply in describing such personalities since they are not separate entities but distinct parts of the same person.

The term currently in vogue for MPD (multiple personality disorder) is DID (dissociative identity disorder). However, I prefer the term MPD.

What is MPD?

MPD happens when a person, unable to process the atrocities she suffers, splits off the memory into an area of her mind removed from her conscious mind. As the abuse continues, more memories split off. It is as though the core person has amnesia concerning these events, being unable to recall at will what she has gone through. These isolated memories usually contain intense emotional trauma and are viewed by the person as being a separate part of herself. Other "personalities" or "alters," as they are sometimes called, may talk, function and have personality traits that are very different from the core person.

I view MPD as God's gift to prevent insanity in children. Just as I affirm the ability of the mind to "dissociate," I also affirm that it is God's will for a person's mind to return to its originally created state—wholeness. How that happens will be addressed later.

Is there any evidence in the Bible that MPD exists?

There are numerous general principles for discerning the reality of something not specifically mentioned in Scripture. To discern with integrity, such questions as the following should be asked: "Does it violate any known biblical principles?" "Is there circumstantial evidence for the reality of its existence?" "What do other godly people say about it?" "Does the Lord confirm to your spirit through prayer that it is a reality?"

For some, the Lord has answered their question, "Is MPD real?" with specific verses that relate to being shattered. For example, one person was given Psalm 86:11-13: *Teach me thy way, O LORD; I will walk in thy truth: unite my heart to fear thy name. I will praise thee, O Lord my God, with all my heart: and I will glorify thy name for evermore. For great is thy mercy toward me: and thou hast delivered my soul from the lowest hell* (KJV). Other encouraging verses may be found in Psalm 109:22, Isaiah 11:12 and Psalm 102:20. It should be noted that one of the Greek words for "heal" is *iaomai* which means "made whole."

How is a ministry to people with MPD different than a ministry to other hurting people?

From my viewpoint, ministering to people with MPD is one of the most rewarding types of ministry. This is because you, as a helper, get a ringside seat to watch God dramatically heal and restore a life. Total recovery from MPD is possible. Both spiritual and emotional dimensions are part of the healing process.

Unlike bipolar illness, which partially or totally involves a chemical imbalance in the brain, MPD involves emotional brokenness. (Sometimes, however, there may be a chemical problem as well as MPD present.) People with MPD are usually very creative people who know that they have a problem and are willing to work at seeing God heal them.

What are the qualifications for working with a person with MPD?

Qualifications for ministry are always a servant's heart, a discerning ear, a teachable spirit and a close walk with the Savior. I am *not* suggesting that we all suddenly begin to do the work of a trained Christian counselor. I am sharing these ideas for use by those who are friends of people with MPD. The loving and helping ministry of a friend may often supplement ministry by a professional counselor.

Why is it that a person may not realize for years that events happened and then suddenly remembers them?

Without going into a complicated discussion about how memories are stored in the brain or the difference between repressed memories and dissociative memories, let me say that a similar phenomenon occurs in war veterans when they dissociate from a terrible memory of something they saw or did. Years later, something may trigger memories of a past event. It is very typical for an abused woman to begin having flashbacks soon after the birth of her first child (especially if it is a girl).

Does a person ever have false memories? Should I always believe what someone is telling me about a memory?

Since Satan is a deceiver, he can no doubt imitate both MPD and supposed memories. Counselors should maintain prayerful carefulness and awareness against being deceived. The Holy Spirit will be faithful to supply a "warning signal" if deception is present. (I should add that, in nearly thirty years of ministering to those with MPD, I have never come across a case of false memories. However, other Christian workers have.)

Be sure to let the person with MPD know that you believe her. Previously, she may have been silenced by being told that *if* she disclosed the abuse she would never be believed anyway. Let the Lord confirm in your heart the truth about her past. Have the person (who may be desperately trying to maintain the inner lie that none of this ever happened) make the affirmation, "I choose to believe only the truth about my past."

What if I can't handle hearing about the terrible atrocities the person wants to tell me?

If you are not a trained Christian counselor, your role may *not* involve the intense memory work that is usually a part of the healing process. However, if it does, be aware that the enemy would like to use the pictures of abuse that are now in *your* mind as a means of personal torment or harassment. Express your concerns about hearing gory details to the person to whom you are ministering. As long as she has an appropriate place to deal with these memories—with a therapist, for example—there is nothing wrong with putting a limit on your involvement with this part of her healing.

However, if you believe that you should be available to work through some of these difficult memories with her, consciously ask the Lord to erase any distressing pictures from your mind. Refuse to allow them to resurface by consciously handing the memory up to the Lord and asking Him to do with it as He pleases.

Do each of the personalities have to be "saved" before full healing can take place?

My answer to this question is a politically correct one: no, but maybe! I believe that a person who has made a commitment to Jesus Christ as her Savior is saved. That salvation results in that person being made alive in her spirit. MPD is an issue of emotional fragmenting; it has nothing to do with the human spirit.

I believe that what some say is an event of leading a non-core personality to the Lord is in actuality the bringing of the reality of the decision previously made for Christ into the conscious reality of the personality. If, for example, a person was saved at age eighteen, those personalities that stopped growing emotionally at age nine may not be aware of the person's decision for Christ which was made at age eighteen. So, is it OK to tell a personality the plan of salvation and lead her in a prayer of faith? Absolutely. God will direct you.

What is integration, and how does it happen?

I define integration, or merging, as I prefer to call it, as "having each part take its rightful place in the person." This eliminates the frightening possibility that the parts or personalities will "die" or "disappear." Integration removes the lie.

There are two ways that integration takes place. *First*, emotional splintering stays in place as long as there are such lies remaining in the system. For example, the lie might be, "That never happened to me." That is why integration may simply occur by telling someone what happened to her. Knowledge, in effect, removes the lie. At other times, there may still be no integration even after the person has remembered a forgotten traumatic event. The memory is still "toxic" to her. In this case, there is probably still a lie connected with that event. For example, the person may remember the event but still believes that it was her fault or that what occurred happened because she was a bad person.

Second, I have seen examples of "delayed integration" where removing the lies and replacing them with the truth didn't seem to bring instantaneous merging. I am not sure why this occurs. There are several possibilities: 1) personalities need to live a safe, normal life for a short time as part of their healing; 2) God simply has His own timing for that part to be merged; or 3) the person herself may need to process all of her emotions.

What are some of the strong points of a person with MPD?

They may seem to hear more clearly or precisely from God than other people do. I believe that this is because, having lived a life that included a spiritual dimension filled with emotional confusion and the reality of wicked spirits and supernatural events, there is special sensitivity or spiritual discernment which could be compared to the extra-sensitive sense of smell or touch some blind people have. It could be too that God in His graciousness speaks clearly to people with MPD so that there will be no confusion about whose voice it is.

What does the term SRA refer to?

SRA is an abbreviation for Satanic Ritual Abuse. It refers to the abuse suffered by those who are forced to participate in rituals related to the worship of Satan.

Is there any evidence in the Bible that SRA really exists?

Many of the elements of occult activity, Satan worship and ritual abuse are described in Scripture. Such things as ceremonial worship rites, sexual perversion, child sacrifice, animal sacrifice and use of psychic (supernatural) powers which can be seen today in ritual abuse situations are repeatedly mentioned in both the Old and New Testaments.

Paul says in First Corinthians 10:20, ". . . but I say that the things which the Gentiles sacrifice, they sacrifice to demons and not to God . . .," making it clear that even in the New Testament the pagan peoples were unknowingly (and perhaps knowingly) involved with demon worship. Three of those central gods (demons) were Molech, Baal and Chemosh. The worship of all three involved atrocities to children. See Appendix A: "A Biblical Basis for Acknowledging the Reality of Satanic Ritual Abuse." (For more information, see *The Bible and the Reality of SRA*, published by Lydia Press.)

If MPD and SRA are a reality, why are some pastors reluctant to take them into account when counseling?

Although many police departments have specially trained units capable of determining if a crime scene has the characteristics of satanic ritual abuse, and some hospitals in major cities have entire floors of their psychiatric units designated for ritual abuse survivors, some believers are unwilling to acknowledge the reality of spiritual warfare, particularly MPD and SRA.

Some churches teach that emotions are "bad" or "corrupt." They believe that "denying self" means to refuse to acknowledge emotions. Since MPD is not viewed as a mental problem but an issue of overwhelming emotions, many pastors are unwilling to deal with it. The Scriptures affirm, however, that all believers are united with Christ and therefore do have authority to address and expel the dark powers.

Some pastors are afraid to deal with issues involving Satan. Perhaps this is due to an unbiblical view of spiritual warfare.

How does a wicked spirit get inside someone?

Satan affects us all from the outside through temptations and trying to get us to believe lying thoughts, etc. He works on a "legal" system. He is able to affect people only when he has been given ground or place or permission to control some part(s) of their lives. Once the door into a person's life has been opened, demonic forces may enter and take up residence. Doors may be opened by the person herself (knowingly or unknowingly), or by someone else (particularly parents or other relatives), through generational covenants, for example. I personally have never worked with a person who had MPD who *did not* have generational issues to address.

How does a "deliverance ministry" fit in with the overall ministry to a person with MPD?

A deliverance ministry should be part of an overall discipleship program. Sometimes, especially where there are generational issues, a person may need help in evicting demonic forces. However, deliverance ministries are sometimes conducted in unscriptural ways. As well, the adrenaline rush of "hand-to-hand combat" with the enemy can be heady stuff, and the battle, not the freedom, may become the focus.

The way a policeman uses his authority is a good example of how we can and should exercise our authority in Christ. The policeman doesn't need to scream or shout or wildly wave his arms as he stands in the street directing traffic. He simply puts up his hand, blows his whistle and motorists obey him. Why? Because the authority of the whole police department is behind him. His badge, a symbol of that authority, is a reminder to all that they must obey. (To "cast out" personalities is disastrous. It is possible that a personality may be agreeing with the darkness to such a degree that a demonic presence as well as the personality may be present. But they are not one and the same. Instead of casting out the personality, ask God to make a space between the personality and the wicked spirit[s] present so that the situation will clarify itself.)

What should I do if a person suddenly becomes another personality as we are talking together?

Pray for guidance and speak with the personality just as you would with any individual. Determine why this personality is "strong" (dominant) at this particular time. (It may be that she is protecting the core person from hearing or feeling something.) If you know that the personality is believing a lie about something she thinks is threatening her or the core person, speak the truth about the specific issue of concern. If it is essential that the core person return and take control, ask if any of the personalities inside knows how to put her back in charge.

What are some of the problems a person with MPD might have in her relationships with others?

Many hurting people, even those without MPD, have had a life of trying to stay alive, both physically and emotionally. This may be especially true of the teen years when social skills would normally develop. As a result, they may have problems establishing healthy relationships with others. For instance, they may tend to take comments or actions personally; they may be overly sensitive to looks or words from others; another person may remind them of their mother or father, and they may project some of those feelings onto the person who wants to be their friend. One way to help teach them social skills is to be a true friend to them. Do not be easily offended, and display a willingness to address issues as they surface.

What does a person with MPD want from me?

They are longing for someone to listen to them, to believe them; someone to let them "borrow hope" when everything seems hopeless; someone to keep their confidences; someone to model the unconditional love of the Father.

How can I avoid having all my time filled with ministry to someone with MPD?

First, make sure that your motives for helping are not clouded by your own needs. For example, avoid ministering because you need to feel needed by someone or because you are a "fix-it" person who can't stand to see messes in other people's lives. Avoid self-reliance, and be very clear about where you believe God would have you put boundaries on your ministry.

Work with the person to make a list of five to seven people whom they can call in an emergency. If the first person is unavailable, out of town or simply busy, encourage the person with MPD to call the next person. Ministry needs to be a team project. It is possible for one person to be easily overwhelmed especially at the beginning stage of recovery.

Is it necessary for each personality to "grow up" to the core person's age before it can be integrated (merged)?

Although some therapists would answer this question positively, I do not think so. From my own experience, as well as from my work with other people with MPD, I have seen instantaneous as well as progressive integration.

How do I help alleviate the person with MPD's fear that she is going crazy or losing her mind?

It is very common for a person to feel that she is going insane even while she is being healed. Part of this is due to the unusual feeling that occurs as different personalities emerge. Constant assurance that she is not going crazy may be needed. I sometimes encourage people by saying, "If you would have gone insane, it would have been back then when you were going through all those terrible things. The fact that you survived those times shows that God has given your mind an incredible ability to stay sane."

I also point out that people who are losing their grip on reality don't know they are! The fact that the person with MPD is concerned about losing her mind is a sign that she is *not* crazy!

What should I do if a person begins to get extremely agitated during a Bible study or class?

Quietly ask her if she would like to go outside with you for some fresh air. Do not touch her. This may startle her and be perceived as a threat. Pray for wisdom, and once outside, tell her you sensed that she was getting upset. Ask how you can help.

Should I be afraid?

No. People with MPD may become extremely angry and emotionally overwhelmed at times. However, such anger is usually directed toward themselves. The only time I have heard of someone with MPD hurting or attacking one who was helping her occurred when the helper made the mistake of trying to physically restrain the person. (The person inadvertently struggled with the helper because she was having a childhood flashback of being held down and hurt by her mother.)

If a personality tells me that she is going to kill herself, what should I do?

One of the main things to remember when helping a person with MPD resist suicide is to assure her that she will always be in control of the situation, i.e., that you will never force her to go anywhere or do anything that she herself does not choose to do. Her past experiences probably never allowed her to be in control. She may have been physically held down, spiritually overwhelmed or emotionally manipulated. Therefore, it is important to stress that she is in charge of her life.

Be honest with your feelings. Say things like, "I would be so sad if you died. You are so special to me." "You're such a fighter and have gone through so much. It would be so sad if you were to give up right before the good part begins." It may also be helpful to point out that the people who abused her in the past would be happy if they knew her life had ended. "Don't let them win," may be a helpful statement.

Ask her if she has told her counselor about wanting to kill herself. Make every effort to convince her to call the counselor, but do not call the counselor without the person's permission. Although this is a controversial point, I do not believe that responsibility should be taken by the helper. The issue of trust is important. Let her know clearly that you will not tell anyone about her situation without her permission. If she will not initially allow you to contact her counselor, keep trying to convince her, or ask if there is anyone inside who wants you to tell someone.

Always pray with her—if she is agreeable. Realize that there may be spiritual issues, lies from demonic forces at work in her. Ask the Lord to give you wisdom as to how to pray specifically for her. A note of encouragement: I believe that people with MPD are one of the least likely populations to actually commit suicide. They are fighters. If that were not the case, they would not have made it this far.

Remember that within yourself you do not have the resources to prevent a suicide. But you do have a lifeline to the One who can!

What if the personality I am helping wants to do juvenile things such as color or read children's books together?

Ask the Lord if it would be a help to do these things with her. Remember that the personalities are emotionally at the developmental age they were when her traumatic experiences occurred. In this regard, I have benefitted greatly from the work of Dr. Jim Wilder in realizing that one of the best ways to help a hurting person mature is to show by your attitude, body language and actions that you "are glad they are." In other words, you are happy to see her, to be with her, because she is of value as a person. Sometimes by doing activities together, this unmet need to be loved and accepted—to be as Jim says, "the sparkle in someone's eye"—finds fulfillment.

What should I do if she screams and runs out of the room?

Don't try to stop her. If you try to prevent her from escaping the room, she may have a flashback to an earlier time that may escalate the situation. Calmly go after her. If possible, do not run—she may think you are chasing her. Quietly talk to the personality that is present, and assure her that she is safe. Ask her what has frightened her.

Are there certain stages a person with MPD goes through in the healing process?

Usually the healing process goes in stages. Perhaps for years the individual has experienced unusual, unexplainable events: loss of time, two different sets of clothing in the closet, people whom she does not know seeming to know her, being told she said (or did) this or that without any memory herself of having said or done it, etc.

When MPD is first suggested as a possible cause for these strange events, the person usually has a hard time believing that this is true. This difficulty in accepting MPD will likely remain—at times stronger than other times—right up until the healing process is completed. This is partially due to the fact that the amnesia about the abuse serves to keep the lie in place: "This didn't happen to me."

In most cases, at the beginning of the healing process the core person doesn't realize when another personality takes over and begins talking. But as the healing progresses, there is a sensation similar to dreaming where the core person may hear or vaguely be aware of what another personality is saying (either within the mind or audibly).

During some part of the healing process, the person may become triggered (and switch to another personality) so often that one personality after another comes "to the top" (as I call it). As the Lord begins to allow the memories to surface, the emotional pain the different personalities hold is expressed, causing emotional upheaval. This is a very difficult time for the person. It presents an opportunity for those around her to assure her of their love and support.

There may come a point in her healing that the person can take on a new role in helping those personalities inside her. If, for example, she realizes that she is suddenly feeling terrified, she may be able to ask those inside what the problem is: "Why are we afraid?" Sometimes they will cooperate by indicating the cause of the terror. The core person can then speak truth to the situation and may not only find relief but may also experience spontaneous merging (integration). For example, if someone inside says, "I'm scared he's going to kill me," the person could ask, "Who's going to kill you?" The answer: "My father." The truth that can be expressed is, "Our father is dead now, and he can't hurt us anymore. Why don't you ask the Lord Jesus what the truth about this is?"

How long does healing usually take?

The healing process is different for each person. In most people's lives the Lord combines spiritual freedom with emotional healing, accomplishing both at the same time. In others, spiritual freedom may be separated by time from emotional healing. (In other words, there may be more of an emphasis on spiritual deliverance at the beginning.)

One of the things that can speed up the healing process is for the person to keep affirming, "I am willing to look at anything from my past that the Lord wants me to look at." Also, "I choose to believe the truth about the past." Both of these statements will help to combat the inner resistance to go back to incredibly painful memories of events from the past.

How do I deal with a personality who is antagonistic to me, to other Christians or to God?

You are not obligated to defend God or answer the "where was He when . . ." question. When confronted with aggressive personalities, I try to remember the incredible hurt that is beneath the anger. (This also keeps me from taking insults personally.) I usually try to get the personality to talk to God about what she thinks of Him. Sometimes this is helpful, sometimes not. I also point out the truth that she must have been very deeply hurt to have so much anger. I tell her that I think she is being tricked into believing lies about God. (In one particularly energy-charged discussion where it was obvious that the personality was agreeing with the demonic forces within, the only break in the antagonistic attitude of the personality came when I said, "I can't understand. You seem like such an intelligent person. I can't figure out why you've chosen the losing side!") Obviously, these answers may not apply to every situation. Ask God for wisdom.

On behalf of folks with MPD, thank you for being willing to be a friend.